CONTENTS

D1542609

Welcome

How do I cultivate a life that is purposeful, deep, and fruitful? What are the commitments, critical risks, and personal practices that open me to God's grace? How can I discover the spiritual life and the difference God intends for me to make in the world?

Radical Hospitality. Passionate Worship. Intentional Faith Development. Risk-Taking Mission and Service. Extravagant Generosity. The fruitful, God-related life develops from intentional and repeated attention to these five essential practices that are critical for our growth in Christ.

Forty Days of Fruitful Living: Practicing a Life of Grace provides readings taken from the book *Five Practices of Fruitful Living* presented in the format of daily devotions for use by individuals, classes, Bible studies, and congregations.

These practices—to receive God's love, to love God in return, to grow in Christ, to serve others, and to give back—are so essential to our growth in Christ that failure to attend to them, develop them, and deepen them limits our capacity to live fruitfully, to settle ourselves completely in God, and to become instruments of God's transforming grace.

Forty Days of Fruitful Living directs us toward the practices that open our hearts to God, to others, and to a life rich with meaning, relationship, and contribution.

How to Use This Book

Forty Days of Fruitful Living: Practicing a Life of Grace is designed to provide a unifying, renewing, outward-focused immersion into the life of grace. If you are using *Forty Days of Fruitful Living* as a Lenten devotion, begin reading on Ash Wednesday. Since Lent includes forty days *plus* Sundays, there are six unnumbered thematic introductions so that you can continue daily work on Sundays, prepare for the week to come, and still finish on Easter weekend.

If you are reading *Forty Days of Fruitful Living* during the fall or summer, simply follow the sequence of numbered readings beginning with the first reading and continuing on to finish in forty days.

For a deeper spiritual exploration, share your thoughts and reflections daily with friends or family members, or keep a journal of your responses. To explore more, I invite you to read the original book, *Five Practices of Fruitful Living*.

I pray that *Forty Days of Fruitful Living* encourages you in your following of Christ and blesses your congregation in the great task of ministry in the spirit of Christ.

Robert Schnase

Christian Practices

Christian practices are those essential activities that create openings for God's Spirit to shape us. The flourishing life results from repeating and deepening these practices and from the lifelong project of cooperating with the Holy Spirit in our own spiritual growth. Practices sharpen our awareness of the spiritual life and help us see the presence of God more clearly in daily life.

Practices express and fulfill our intention to become a different kind of person because of our following in the way of Jesus. As we learn to listen for God, to invite God in, and work with God, our lives are shaped. God uses our efforts to change us from the inside out. We become new creations in Christ, and we arrive at places we never expected.

Day One

"I am the vine, you are the branches." —John 15:5

Jesus taught a way of life and invited people into a relationship with God that was vibrant, dynamic, and fruitful. He said, "I am the vine, you are the branches. Those who abide in me and I in them bear much fruit. . . . My father is glorified by this, that you bear much fruit and become my disciples" (John 15:5, 8). Jesus wanted people to flourish.

Scripture is sprinkled with phrases that point to fruitful living—the kingdom of God, eternal life, immeasurable riches, a peace that passes all understanding, abundant life.

Jesus and his followers developed core fundamental spiritual practices that sustained them in God and motivated them to relieve the burdens that restrain people from flourishing by protecting the vulnerable, embracing outcasts, healing the sick, welcoming children, caring for widows, confronting injustice, pardoning sin, preaching good news, releasing people from the fear of death. They presented the gift and demand of God's grace to everyone. They granted peace. Paul writes, "Let the same mind be in you that was in Christ Jesus" (Philippians 2:5). Scripture is unified around the theme of a vibrant, fruitful, dynamic life with God through following Christ.

How do I have the mind in me that was in Christ? How do I cultivate a life that is abundant, fruitful, purposeful, and deep? What are the commitments, critical risks, and practices that open me to God's transforming grace, and that help me discover the difference God intends for me to make in the world? How do I live the fruitful, flourishing life of a follower of Christ?

The fruitful, God-related life develops with intentional, sustained attention to five essential practices that are critical for our growth in Christ. *Radical Hospitality* in our personal walk with Christ begins with an extraordinary receptivity to the grace of God. We invite God into our hearts and make space for God in our lives. We receive God's love.

Through the practice of *Passionate Worship*, we learn to love God in return. We practice listening for God, allowing God to shape our hearts and minds through prayer, devotion, and worship. We love God in return.

Through the practice of *Intentional Faith Development*, we do the soul work that connects us to others, immerses us in God's Word, and positions us to grow in grace and mature in Christ. We learn in community.

Risk-Taking Mission and Service involves offering ourselves in purposeful service to others in need, making a positive difference even at significant personal cost and inconvenience to ourselves. We serve others.

Through the practice of *Extravagant Generosity*, we offer our material resources in a manner that supports the causes that transform life and relieve suffering, and that enlarges our soul and sustains the spirit. We give back.

These Five Practices—to receive God's love, to love God in return, to grow in Christ, to serve others, and to give back—are so essential to growth in Christ and to the deepening of the spiritual life that failure to attend to them, develop them, and deepen them with intentionality limits our capacity to live fruitfully and fully, to settle ourselves completely in God, and to become instruments of God's transforming grace. The adjectives—*radical, passionate, intentional, risk-taking*, and *extravagant*—provoke us out of complacency and remind us that these practices require more than haphazard, infrequent, and mediocre attention. Cultivating our relationship with God requires our utmost and highest.

These practices open our heart—to God, to others, to a life that matters. They help us to live a life of grace.

Read John 15:1-17.

Abundant life, the kingdom of God, eternal life, immeasurable riches, internal peace, a life of grace—what comes to mind when you reflect on these things? What kind of life does God desire for us? How can we have in us "the mind that was in Christ"?

Prayer: Lord, lead me to the rediscovery of wonder, awe, peace, joy, life. Help me find myself, my true self, in following you.

2

Day Two

"Be doers of the word, and not merely hearers . . ." —James 1:22

Picture the graceful performance of a gymnast. With effortless elegance, she balances on the high beam, lifting herself up on a single tiptoe and down again, bows low with arms gracefully outstretched. Her ease of movement, naturalness of posture, and energetic responses make her look entirely at home balancing on a beam only a few inches wide. She bends and stretches in ways that defy ordinary human athleticism, occasionally suspending herself steadily on one hand or two, other times leaping high above the beam as if free of gravity itself. She smiles, breathing easily and smoothly, as if the workout has barely challenged her.

How does she make it look so natural? It looks so easy precisely because she has worked so hard. She has repeated and practiced and rehearsed the hundreds of small incremental motions for years that combine to make possible such ease of movement. What seemed at first to be impossible, or extraordinarily difficult, became progressively easier and more satisfying through months and years of practice. It was not easy or natural until, through repetition, the muscles themselves developed the memory that the art requires. Hundreds of hours of effort, commitment, and practice prepared her to perform so naturally and gracefully.

Or watch young Little League baseball players practice. They scoop up ground balls, catch pop-up flies, throw the ball around the bases, and practice batting.

Now watch professional baseball players practice before a Major League game. These players are paid handsomely; they are elite athletes at the height of their careers. What do they do to practice before each Major League game? They scoop up grounders, catch pop-ups, throw the ball around the bases, and practice batting.

Baseball involves certain fundamental activities, and every play of every game involves those basic elements performed with endless variations. A player simply keeps repeating and improving on the same basic elements. No professional baseball player says, "I don't practice batting anymore because I learned that in high school."

Christian practices are those essential activities we repeat and deepen over time. They create openings for God's Spirit to shape us. They are not steps that we complete and put behind us never to repeat again. And practices are not static qualities that some people naturally possess and others absolutely lack. Anyone can start at any point and at any level and begin to develop the practices; with the help of the Holy Spirit, the practices will change who they are. Practices are not simply principles we talk about; practices are something we do.

Through practices we become "doers of the word, and not merely hearers" (James 1:22), and we weave together faith and action, theology and life, thinking and doing, intention and realization, heart and head with hands. Practices make our faith a tangible and visible part of daily life. We see them done in the life of Jesus, and we do them until they become a way of life for us. Even when we cannot articulate the content of our faith with confidence or detail, through our practice we embody faith and express our ultimate commitment to God and our desire to follow Christ. Practices represent our positive contribution to the transformation of all things through Christ.

Through practice, we open ourselves to grace and let ourselves be opened by grace. We follow Christ, step by step, day by day, again and again; and by these steps and through these days, we are changed, we become someone different, we become new creations in Christ.

Read James 1:22-27.

How do you think practice deepens the spiritual life? What patterns of spiritual practice already characterize your life? How does God use these to shape you?

Prayer: Help me both hear your word and act on it so my life serves you and I am not self-deceived, my God. Don't let me be fooled into merely listening without acting on your truth.

3
Day Three

Jesus said to him, "I am the way, and the truth, and the life."
—John 14:6

The ministry of Jesus is grounded in personal practices. Jesus' life is marked by prayer, solitude, worship, reflection, the study of Scripture, conversation, community, serving, engagement with suffering, and generosity. These personal practices sustained a ministry that opened people to God's grace, transformed human hearts, and changed the circumstances of people in need. Jesus modeled going away to quiet places, spending time in the Temple, and listening for God. Jesus spoke to the woman at the well, the tax collector in the tree, the rich young ruler on the road, the paralyzed man beside the pool, to the lepers and the blind and the widowed and the wealthy, to Mary and Martha and Peter and John. He held a child in his arms, noticed the woman who touched his robe, healed a soldier's servant, ate with sinners, told stories to Pharisees, and blessed the thief beside him on the cross. He intervened to challenge unjust systems that abused vulnerable people, overturning the money changers' tables and dispersing those ready to kill a woman accused of adultery. He connected people to God, opened their hearts and minds to God's kingdom, invited them to follow in his steps, and set them on a path toward God. Jesus knitted them into community, interlaced their lives with one another by the Holy Spirit, and wove them into the body of Christ, the church. By example and story, by lessons and parables, and by inviting them into ministry and sending them out in his name, he taught them to practice and live the ways of God. Jesus made maturing in faith and growth toward God unexpectedly and irresistibly appealing.

Christianity began as a way of life rather than as a system of beliefs, the way taught and modeled by Jesus Christ.

By repeating and deepening certain fundamental practices, we cooperate with God in our own growth in Christ and participate with the Holy Spirit in our own spiritual maturation. The fundamental practices are rooted in Scripture and derived from the clear imperatives of the life of Christ; they are distilled through the monastic formative exercises of the early church and are sharpened by the community disciplines of the early Methodists and other renewal movements. They find expression today in congregations throughout the world that intentionally cultivate authentic life in Christ and the formation of Christian character and service.

The Five Practices invite us along a pathway prepared by hundreds of generations that embeds us in community, connects us with God, and provides avenues for us to make a difference. They re-enchant the world for us. They tumble us headlong into the mystery of life.

When Jesus said, "I am the way, and the truth, and the life" (John 14:6), he was not speaking arrogantly, egotistically, or narrow-mindedly. He was expressing a genuine desire to turn us, to redirect us away from things that do not satisfy and toward the things that cause us to come alive. The time given to us on this earth is infinitesimally small compared to time itself, and so he desires for us to live it richly. Jesus asks us to build our houses upon solid rock rather than shifting sand. He invites us. He wants us to flourish.

Read 1 John 4:7-16.

What persons have lived the kind of life that makes you want to be like them in character, graciousness, generosity? How did they become like that? How did they cooperate with God in their own growth in Christ? How do practices turn us toward Christ?

Prayer: Stay with me, Lord, in my following of the way you have shown me. May your love become real in me, not disappearing from sight but becoming audible and visible in my words and actions.

4

Day Four

*"So this is my prayer: that your love will flourish. . . . Live a
lover's life, circumspect and exemplary, a life Jesus will be proud
of: bountiful in fruits from the soul, making Jesus Christ
attractive to all, getting everyone involved in the glory and praise
of God." —Philippians 1:9, 11,* The Message

The Christian life is a gift of God, an expression of God's grace in
Christ, the result of an undeserved and unmerited offering of love
toward us. Every step of the journey toward Christ is preceded by,
made possible by, and sustained by the perfecting grace of God.

However, becoming the person that God desires us to become is
also the fruit of a persistent and deeply personal quest, an active desire
to love God, to allow God's love to lead us. The fruitful life is cultivated by placing ourselves in the most advantageous places to see,
receive, learn, and understand the love that has been offered in Christ.

So deeply is the notion of Christian practices embedded in our faith
tradition that the name of the Book of Acts in the original Greek is
praxeis, from which we derive our word *practice*. In the second chapter
of the Acts (practices!) of the Apostles, Luke reminds us that the essential activities of Christian living include worshipping God, learning
God's Word, serving one another, and sharing generously. The
repeated pattern of these practices formed the early Christian church
into a community that was so appealing in its purpose and its conduct
of life together, that people were added to their number day by day.

The patristic and monastic teachers of the early church developed
rich disciplines of daily practice that included hospitality and receptivity; worship and prayer; study and learning in community; service
to the ill, poor, and imprisoned; and the stewardship of all earthly
possessions. Daily and consistent practice helped Christ's followers

accomplish the tasks given by God for the fruitful life. "Christian formation" describes the way our intentionally repeated activities help us cooperate with the Holy Spirit in God's "forming" of us into new creatures.

The early Methodist movement thrived under the rubrics of personal practices—worship, singing, fasting, and receiving the sacraments; searching Scripture and participating in classes and covenant groups for spiritual encouragement and accountability; serving the poor and visiting the sick and imprisoned; and tithing their incomes. John Wesley's was a theology of *grace*, focused on God's initiating love in Christ. The Methodist renewal, however, rested on *practices*, emphasizing the role we play in our own spiritual growth and the perfecting role of community to shape us. Early Wesleyans were chided as "Methodists" because of their nearly eccentric adherence to methodical ways of systemizing the practices of the Christian faith to promote learning, service, and growth in Christ through daily and weekly exercises and patterns.

Some people enter the journey with Christ through service; others through a growing sense of belonging. Small steps in one area are followed by giant leaps in another; there is ebb and flow, growth and setback, detour and recalibration. These are the essential practices that move us along the path in following Christ; nevertheless, no two journeys look exactly the same. Fruitful living is "a garden with a thousand gates."[1]

God loves us and desires a relationship with us. Loving God in return changes us. Growing in grace deepens our experience of living. Serving others gives us something to live for. Living well involves keeping these truths in sharp awareness. The Five Practices take us to the things that last.

Read Philippians 2:1-13.

Who were you ten years ago in terms of character compared to who you are today? Who do you hope to be in terms of character and spirit ten years from now? How do you let God change you?

Prayer: Reach down to me just where I am, Lord, and help me flourish in my following in your way as I take the next step toward you. Grant me patience and perseverance as I practice your love so that things I formerly thought impossible become real in me in my daily life.

Receiving God's Love

THE PRACTICE OF RADICAL HOSPITALITY

The practice of *Radical Hospitality* in our personal walk with Christ begins with an extraordinary receptivity to the grace of God. In distinctive and personal ways, we invite God into our hearts and say *Yes* to God's initiating grace. *Hospitality* toward God means we welcome God in, receive God's love, and make room for God in our lives. We cultivate a pattern of opening the door to the spiritual life rather than closing it, of saying *Yes* to God's desire to have a relationship with us.

Radical derives from the word "root," and describes a profound, deep-rooted receptivity that exceeds ordinary patterns. Those who practice *Radical Hospitality* invite God into the core of their existence; seeking God becomes a fundamental and defining element of their lives.

During the next several days, focus on receiving God's love. Approach this week with an open heart, an exploring curiosity, and an invitational attitude toward God. Allow yourself to be struck by grace!

Dear God, help me reach for you
as you are reaching for me.

Day Five

"We love because he first loved us." —1 John 4:19

"Accept that you are accepted." When I read this as a college student, those words by Paul Tillich jolted me into a new understanding of God's unconditional love.[2] The pivotal first element in our walk of faith—the practice of Radical Hospitality—involves our saying *Yes* to God's love for us, a willingness to open our lives to God and invite God into our hearts. It involves our capacity to receive grace, accept Christ's love, and make room for God in our lives.

"Do we know what it means to be struck by grace?" Tillich asks. This was a provocative notion to me, an odd metaphor, to describe God's grace as something that strikes, that jars us into a new way of thinking, that collides with our old way of being. He continues, "We cannot transform our lives, unless we allow them to be transformed by that stroke of grace." The first movement toward the transformed life and becoming the person God wants us to be begins when we face the startling reality of God's unconditional love for us. Receiving the love and forgiveness of God and opening ourselves to the new life it brings can be as abrupt as lightening striking across the black night sky. It means we've been struck by grace.

The personal practice of Radical Hospitality begins with a receiving, perceiving, listening, opening, accepting attitude—a readiness to accept and welcome God's initiative toward us. It is sustained with active behaviors that place us in the most advantageous posture to continue to receive God, welcome Christ, and make room for grace. And so it involves interior decision and soul work, a listening and receptivity to God, as well as habits that transform us as we regularly, frequently, and intentionally make room in our lives for God.

Grace strikes at unexpected times, Tillich suggests: when we are in pain, feeling restless, empty, alone. When the ordinariness of life grinds us down, or the vacuity of the world's promises leaves us empty, when we finally realize our churning and churning is taking us nowhere fast, in such moments, grace comes to us like a wave of light in the darkness, and we perceive a voice saying, "You are accepted." We don't have to give anything; only to receive what is given. Our only and singular task is to *accept* that we are accepted.

You are *loved*. You *are* loved. *You* are loved.

Can you accept that?

God's love for us is not something we have to strive for, earn, work on, or fear. It is freely given. That is key: that we are loved, first, finally, and forever by God, a love so deep and profound and significant that God offers his Son to signify and solidify this love forever so that we get it. When we finally do get it, and open our hearts to the truth of God's love for us, we begin to receive glimpses of a peace that the world cannot give or take away, an inner assurance about our ultimate worth in God's eyes that surpasses understanding.

The journey to becoming what God would have us to be begins with opening ourselves to this love and giving it a place in our hearts. The welcoming requires of us an extraordinary hospitality, a radical receptivity, a willingness to allow God to come in and dwell within our hearts.

Accept that you are accepted. In the moment that grace strikes, grace conquers sin. Grace helps us face the truth about ourselves, to embrace it rather than run from it; and by embracing this truth and offering it to God, we discover that God knows the truth about us and still loves us, and that God will shape us from this day forward anew. God's been waiting for us, desiring us to let him in.

Accept that you are accepted. Open the doors of your heart.

Read 1 John 4:7-12.

Who are some people God has used to express God's unconditional love for you? In what ways do you feel like you invite God in and make room for God's love in your life?

Prayer: Spirit of the Living God, fall afresh on me. Break open my heart with your love. Help me practice real love instead of just talking about love so that I can truly live.

6

Day Six

"For by grace you have been saved through faith, and this is not your own doing; it is the gift of God." —Ephesians 2:8

Can you remember one moment in your life that changed all the others? Accepting that you are accepted can be such a moment. Being struck by grace can prove such a time. Inviting God in alters everything. Love changes us, and through us, it changes others around us.

Scripture tells many stories of unexpected grace. Saul on the Damascus road, Zacchaeus, Mary Magdalene, the woman beside the well, the worshipful Mary and her obsessive sister Martha, the man paralyzed beside the pool, the woman accused of adultery, the soldier with a dying servant, the thief on the cross—what happened to them all? Struck by grace, penetrated by the unfathomable and overwhelming truth of God's love for them, they opened their hearts to God and invited God in.

Through Jesus, God said *Yes* to them, and each in her or his own way found the courage to say *Yes* to God; and in that interchange, all things became new. God's welcoming of them was met with a new hospitality toward God.

God's love has a piercing quality, a persevering element, an assertive and searching aspect. God's grace has the generative power to pardon, transform, redeem, and perfect, and it pushes and pursues. It's not that we love first, but that we are first loved. This active, reaching quality of God's love is what *grace* refers to, a gift-like initiative on God's part toward us.

Paul writes, "For by *grace* you have been *saved* through *faith*, and this is not your own doing; it is the gift of God" (Ephesians 2:8, emphasis added). *Saved* means that we come into a right relationship with God, becoming what God created us to be. *Saved* refers to our becoming whole, our living fully and abundantly the fruitful life. Paul says there are two essential and operative elements to this whole and right relationship with God, *grace* and *faith*.

Grace refers to the gift-like quality of God's love, the initiating power and presence of God in our lives. *Grace* is God accepting us, despite our rejecting or ignoring or rebelling against God's love. *Grace* is God offering us a relationship, loving us. It is the unexpected UPS package delivered to our front door with our name on it.

Faith is our acceptance of the gift, the opening of our hearts to invite God's love into our lives. *Faith* is our receiving God's grace, love, and pardon, and allowing these gifts to shape us and make us anew. *Faith* is the commitment again and again to live by grace, to honor the gift, and use it, and pass it along. *Faith* is accepting the UPS package, signing on the dotted line, taking it inside our house, unwrapping it, and discovering its treasure.

God's gracious love for us, and the capacity for that love to change our lives when we open ourselves to it, and through us to change the world—this is the central story of the Christian journey. "For God so loved the world that he gave his only Son, so that everyone who believes in him may not perish but may have eternal life" (John 3:16). This verse, the "Gospel in Miniature," captures the interchange between grace and faith and the new life it brings. The God we see revealed in Jesus is the God of *grace*, an active, searching, embracing, assertive love.

The most important journey you will ever take begins by saying *Yes*, by receiving God's love and accepting God's acceptance of you. With lives filtered through a promise, the followers of Jesus live sustained by the assurance of God's unending love. A continuing receptivity to God's initiative in our lives is the key to all the practices that lead to fruitful living.

God loves you. This is the story of grace.

Read Luke 19:1-9.

Have you experienced a time in your life when unexpected love changed you? Through what persons or events have you experienced the initiating, searching quality of God's love?

Prayer: Lord, open my eyes to the striking power of your grace at work in me and in the lives of others around me. Your unexpected love restores me and brings me back to myself.

7

Day Seven

"Do not be conformed to this world, but be transformed by the renewing of your minds, so that you may discern what is the will of God—what is good and acceptable and perfect." —Romans 12:2

God loves you, and this changes everything. If this is so, why is it difficult for us to hear and accept this truth?

An interesting contradiction puzzles sociologists and psychologists. Since World War II, we've faced a time of unprecedented prosperity and material well-being in Western societies. We've had more liberty, more choices, more options, more mobility, and more freedom from fear than at any time in history.[3] So, why have we not been happier? Why have nearly all measures of contentedness, connection, and a sustaining sense of purpose declined?

Cultural voices replay the myth that a good life comes from buying, possessing, and accumulating, and this fosters a thin, elusive, transient, watery happiness. Like a magnet beside a compass that draws the needle away from its true bearing, these cultural voices make it hard for us to move in directions that are positive, that lead to peace and happiness, or that open us to the spiritual life. The thick, rich, lasting notion of a good life, of life abundant and fruitful, comes from deeper sources. It grows from the awareness that God loves us, and from the persistent soul work, the repeated opening of ourselves to God to let ourselves be changed, and from loving and being loved by others. This alone stands as the unassailable and intrinsic source of our living happily, peacefully, and fruitfully.

And the rapid speed and intensity of our high-tech and mobile lifestyles distract us from fathoming the spiritual life and the depth of God's love for us. Intuitively, we know that this type of living does not lead to the rich-textured life that ultimately satisfies. We perceive the difference between living thinly, and living deeply, fruitfully, and abundantly. Life lived entirely on the superficial level lacks depth, purpose, connection. Like water bugs skimming on the surface of a pool, we can live oblivious to the depth and height and expanse of existence.

We also create our own obstacles to God's grace. We willfully deny God's gracious offer of love. By our own attitudes and behaviors we resist grace and its implications that would change us, and avoid real engagement with the interior life and its truths.

Jesus tells three stories in Luke 15 that capture our disconnection from God's searching grace. The first is about Distraction. People are like sheep who distractedly nibble their way lost, mindlessly moving from one green tuft of grass to another until they are somewhere they never intended. The second is about Clutter. Why did the woman have such a difficult time finding the lost coin in her own home? Was her environment so cluttered, so crowded that what she valued could no longer be seen without effort? The third is about Willful Rebellion. The prodigal son runs away from his father, consciously complicit in his own self-destructive impulses.

In addition, internal pressures complicate receiving God's love—negative family voices that replay through our minds, distorting our ability to absorb the truth that God loves us. Part of every childhood involves balancing the signs of parental love and approval with the expressions of disappointment, disapproval, and disinterest that we perceive. Many of us grew up convinced that we are not good enough, smart enough, important enough, athletic enough, or attractive enough to receive the love and affirmation we need or desire. Love, even from parents, seems to have a conditional edge to it, more present when we excel, win, or achieve than when we fail, stumble, struggle, or go our own way. Such unresolved personal issues block our ability to receive true unconditional love from God.

These unmet yearnings make it difficult for us to open ourselves to the truth that God's love is not something we have to struggle for.

Read Luke 15.

What makes it difficult for you to open yourself to the truth of God's love for you? What distracts you from the spiritual life or clutters the way to God for you?

Prayer: Forgive me, Lord, for the many ways I neglect you and shut you out, and for all that obscures your great hope and love for me and others. Find me once again, and bring me home to you.

8

Day Eight

*"Listen! I am standing at the door, knocking; if you hear my
voice and open the door, I will come in to you and eat with you,
and you with me." —Revelation 3:20*

Joe Eszterhas's successful films won awards and earned him millions. But even with throat cancer destroying his larynx, he could not shake his lifelong and life-threatening addictions to alcohol and tobacco. One hot sunny day, trying to outwalk fear, panic, and death, he sat down on the curb, sweating, crying, hyperventilating. He listened to himself moaning, and he heard himself mumble something.

> I couldn't believe I'd said it. . . . Then I listened to myself say it again. And again and again. . . . *"Please, God, help me."* I was praying. Asking. Begging. For help. . . . And I thought to myself: *"Me? Asking God? Begging God? Praying?"* I hadn't even thought about God since I was a boy. . . . And suddenly my heart was stilled. . . . I stopped trembling and twitching.

As he rose to return home, he realized he was not alone, *"I thought I could do it now. . . .* It would be excruciatingly difficult, but with God's help, I thought I could do it." Eszterhas doesn't know whether to describe his experience as God finding him, or him finding God. That day he accepted God's acceptance of himself. It was a day of grace.[4]

Beneath the daily surface life, there continually streams a spiritual dimension, an interior life, a richly sacred and eternal depth. In unexpected moments, events press us deeper than the superficial and invite us to search for answers to questions we haven't even thought to ask before. These moments mark the intersection of daily life and the life of the spirit, the interweaving of the mundane with the sacred, the intermingling of the immediate practical questions of getting along with the deeper questions of direction and purpose.

Some of those moments include a serious health threat, the birth of a child, the death of a family member or close friend, a national tragedy or natural disaster, a painful reversal at work or an unanticipated success, the start or end of a relationship. Such events cause us to question what lasts.

These moments create openings, make us aware of our yearning, and place us in a posture of curiosity and desire. They make us willing to open the door to God's love and ready to receive what God's grace may mean for our lives.

We never earn enough, do enough, or achieve enough to guarantee happiness. And contrary to self-help books, the good life cannot come from inside us by our own efforts. We do not achieve it by trying harder, pushing further, pulling ourselves up by our own bootstraps. Self-love, self-absorption, and self-focus do not take us there.

The good life comes from the practice of hospitality toward God, opening ourselves to God, and making room in our hearts for the gift-like transformation God's love makes possible. Happiness results from patterns of living that draw us closer to God and one another, from practices that open and reopen the connections that bind us to God and to the community. We flourish as we learn to love and be loved, and to serve and be served.

Hospitality toward God opens us to new life. In the practice of making space for God in our hearts again and again, we accept God's gift of new life.

Read Acts 9:1-19.

What unexpected moments or situations have brought you to a new or deeper receptivity to God and God's grace?

Prayer: Take up residence in my life, Lord. Create in me a clean heart, and put within me a new and right spirit. Move in, and make me alive.

9

Day Nine

*"So if anyone is in Christ, there is a new creation: everything old
has passed away; see, everything has become new!"*
—2 Corinthians 5:17

Mitch grew up with no faith background. His alcoholic father was arrested for stealing money and was discovered having an extramarital affair, causing Mitch to have to change schools as a consequence of his parents' divorce. Mitch lost his friends, the job he loved, and his place on the baseball team. He developed a violent temperament and made his own way in a tough world of sports, drinking, and hard living. His envy toward others ate at him. He was angry about things that would never be resolved.

Mitch developed a tough veneer that hid any deeper sense of compassion. He had no faith, no church, no God, and no positive models for how to handle his life. He worked as a truck driver until he saved enough money to pay his way through college. Then Mitch met a young woman who was committed to her faith. In preparation for their marriage, he had several conversations with her pastor, who he came to respect. When Mitch married, he decided that he would "try church." "Is this for real?" was the inner question he wrestled with during his early hesitating steps toward faith. For months he attended with his wife, finding the worship service a confusing litany of language, images, and prayers. He felt like an outsider, but he was determined to make it work.

He and his wife connected with a Sunday school class for young couples. Mitch was invited to help at a community soup kitchen that serves the homeless, and he accepted. He found these strangely satisfying, but he continued to feel turned off by small-minded attitudes and cliquishness. Mitch began to read the Bible, to experiment with praying, to volunteer a little more here and there.

Mitch experienced a deepening of his faith through the weekend adult retreat called *Walk to Emmaus*. He committed to the in-depth DISCIPLE Bible study, and eventually became a Bible study teacher himself. Through his nonjudgmental approach toward people, he became instrumental in helping many unchurched people get involved in various ministries.

Mitch's language is still rough, his manner brusque, and his approach to church and tolerance for protocol are, shall we say, less traditional. But when someone is going through a difficult time, he gives them his phone number and tells them to call him anytime, anywhere, and he'll come. Mitch believes the church really does change lives.

The apostle Paul writes, "So if anyone is in Christ, there is a new creation: everything old has passed away; see, everything has become new!" (2 Corinthians 5:17).

Mitch is a new creation. By the grace of God, Mitch has become someone different from the life that was scripted for him. Through faith in Christ, formed and cultivated through fifteen years of worship, learning, and service, Mitch has found the power to avoid the destructive impulses that undid his father and derailed his family of origin.

Throughout Mitch's life, there were many signs of receptivity, moments when he could have said *No*, but instead said *Yes* on the spiritual journey. Each moment was a sign of his hospitality toward God and of a willingness to allow God to enter in. At each key point, he received God, opened himself to the spiritual life, and welcomed God to play a larger role in his life. Following Christ has been a continuing lifelong process of opening his heart to God.

Read 2 Corinthians 5:17-20.

At what points have you said Yes *to God when you could have said* No, *and saying* Yes *has made all the difference?*

Prayer: Give me a fresh start; create me new. You are the potter, Lord, and I am the clay. Mold me to your purpose. Make me your own.

10

Day Ten

Nathanael said to him, "Can anything good come out of Nazareth?"
Philip said to him, "Come and see." —John 1:46

The personal practice of Radical Hospitality begins with accepting God's love for us offered through Christ, and deciding to let that gracious love make a difference in our lives. It's an attitude; a mindset; an openness to spiritual things; a willingness to listen, perceive, and receive God's presence and initiative. The decision to receive God marks the start of our own journey and soul work, the first step toward a dynamic and vibrant life with God. It involves the critical decision, "Will I open the door to the spiritual life or leave it closed? Will I listen for God, invite God into my heart, and allow God's grace to shape my life, or not?" When we adopt this attitude of acceptance, and say *Yes* to God's initiating grace, we begin down a path that is presently unknown to us and that only becomes knowable as time unfolds.

The personal practice of Radical Hospitality involves both the attitude of receptivity and intentional practice. People who cultivate receptivity look for ways to invite God in rather than to close God out. They regularly ask for God's help, simply and humbly. They desire God's presence. They invite interruptions by God into their lives, interventions of the Spirit, unexpected opportunities for doing what is life-giving.

People who demonstrate the quality of hospitality toward God are curious about God, spirituality, and the interior life. They desire to *know God* rather than merely to know *about God*.

Many of us often approach the spiritual life the way we would an interesting hobby or constructive pastime. We attend church when it's convenient, we pick up some helpful insights and enjoy the people, and we serve on committees to help the organization run smoothly.

Church, religion, and the spiritual life provide some benefit; but we remain puzzlingly remote from real interior work, mystery, or notions of grace. Practicing religion in this way *confirms* something about ourselves rather than *transforming* the nature of who we are.

Even with many years of church experience, many of us may find ourselves still standing on the front porch of the life that is possible in Christ because we've never fully entered in. Or to change the metaphor, we may have left God standing on the front porch of our lives without fully receiving him. We've left undiscovered the "immeasurable riches of God's grace" and "a peace that surpasses all understanding."

People who practice Radical Hospitality toward God move beyond a tentative willingness to sample faith; they actively demonstrate an intentional receptivity to God. They allow God to become a principal part of their life and they become part of God's life. They lay open their hearts.

Those who practice Radical Hospitality invite God into the core of their existence; seeking God becomes a fundamental and defining element of their existence. They realize that deepening the spirit does not come quickly, that following Jesus can be inconvenient, and that gradually surrendering control to God is uncomfortable.

People who practice receptivity realize that following Christ requires deliberate, continuing cooperation with God. They practice, repeat, and deepen the core essentials that open themselves to God. They want God to change them, to make them anew. A God-related life becomes an important stabilizing and orienting force. Growing in Christ becomes an objective. They strive to love the things God loves, to want the things God wants, to find happiness in the things God gives, to find meaning in God's work.

Accept that you are accepted. The first step toward fruitful living involves saying *Yes* to God's unconditional love toward us. God's love changes everything.

Read John 1:43-51.

How do your present patterns of living invite God in or cause you to avoid the spiritual life? What steps can you take to reshape your life toward greater receptivity? How do you plan to say Yes *to God's grace today?*

Prayer: God, help me love the things you love and want the things you want. Get me walking in your way. Open my heart to love the people you have placed in my life.

Loving God in Return

THE PRACTICE OF PASSIONATE WORSHIP

Through the practice of *Passionate Worship*, we learn to love God in return. We practice listening to God, allowing God to shape our hearts and minds through prayer, personal devotion, and community worship.

Passion means full of life, involving our whole selves— mind, body, and spirit. *Passion* means inflamed with love, and refers to our desire to open ourselves entirely to God, inviting God's Spirit to permeate us completely. Through *Passionate Worship* we love God in return, and through our continuing practice we stay in love with God.

For the next several days, we focus on patterns of prayer and worship and how God uses our practice of loving God to form us. Worship connects us to the source of life and helps us grow in Christ.

Prepare for this theme by reflecting on your own experience of worship. What aspects of worship shape your spiritual life the most?

Lord, I surrender my heart to you.

11

Day Eleven

"How lovely is your dwelling place,
O Lord of hosts!
My soul longs, indeed it faints
for the courts of the Lord;
my heart and my flesh sing for joy
to the living God." —Psalm 84:1-2

Linda was in her early forties when her husband died, leaving her the task of raising two young children by herself. Neither her own family nor her husband's were church people, but a few years after her husband's death, her daughters began attending youth activities at a church with their friends. Today, they were singing in the youth choir at the Sunday service, and Linda wanted to be present to support them.

With no church background, attending worship was daunting to her. When she walked in the door, several people offered greetings, shook her hand, and gave her leaflets. She wasn't sure where she was supposed to go and so she stood awkwardly watching the flow of people. As she entered the sanctuary, almost every pew already had people sitting at the ends, and she wasn't sure if she was supposed to step over them or ask them to move down to make room for her. But she persevered and found a place near the back.

As the time for the service approached, music began and people quieted down. She sorted through the announcements about upcoming events. Some piqued her curiosity—a recovery workshop, a financial management class, a Habitat for Humanity project—and others remained a mystery to her, their purpose hidden behind acronyms she didn't understand, such as the Acts 28 Team and an Alpha-Omega Circle meeting. A pastor began to speak, and for several minutes everything seemed a confusing mix of announcements, greetings, and quotes from Scripture. During the prayers, someone mentioned a family by name that had lost a loved one and requested prayers for them. There was silence as people throughout the sanctuary focused on the grieving family. Linda remembered how alone she felt when her husband had died, and she wondered how it must feel to be surrounded by people who are praying for you. "What do the prayers do?" she wondered. She felt moved by the compassion of the gesture.

At last the youth choir moved forward, and she saw her daughters singing with their friends. A sense of parental satisfaction surged through her as she listened. The refrain was beautiful and catchy. She liked it. Later, the pastor told a story about a shepherd leaving the flock behind to search for the sheep that had gone astray. He said that the sheep had "nibbled its way lost," and Linda smiled at the line. That's how we get lost from God, the pastor said. We don't intend to, but we go from one tuft of grass to another until we end up somewhere we never imagined. And yet God loves us and searches for us and never gives up on any one of us. While Linda wasn't sure what she believed about God, the message made her think about her own life.

As the service ended, the mother of one of her daughters' friends came up to Linda and apologized for not noticing her sooner, gave her a gentle hug, and said how glad she was to see her. "Next time you're here, let's sit together," the woman said. Something washed over Linda in that moment that was sudden and profound. The words touched her. She had never imagined returning for worship before that moment. As if a thread of grace had been cast across a great chasm, she felt a connection ever so tenuous and yet full of promise. She returned to her car and sat there for several minutes. "What do I do with this?" she asked herself. "What just happened?" The refrains of her daughters' voices were running through her mind, she was actually praying for a grieving family she didn't even know, she was thinking about that sheep nibbling its way lost, and she was smiling about the invitation to return.

Read Psalm 84.

What are your earliest memories of worship? What made the greatest impression on you? Do you enjoy worship? What causes you delight?

Prayer: Renew me in my love for you, Lord, so that my worship is neither dry nor empty, but full of devotion, eagerness, and joy. I long to live in you, and for you to live in me.

12

Day Twelve

"For all who exalt themselves will be humbled, but all who humble themselves will be exalted." —Luke 18:14

Worship expresses our love for God, our devotion to the creator, redeemer, and sustainer of life. Our response to God's great love for us is to love others and to serve them, and also to express our adoration to God. We love God in return. We open ourselves to God's Spirit so we can see the world through God's eyes. A sustained pattern and practice of worship lends coherence, meaning, depth, and connection to our lives. Worship connects us to God.

Worship changes us. Understanding the meaning of worship requires looking beyond what people do to see with the eyes of faith what God does. God uses worship to crack open closed hearts, reconcile broken relationships, renew hope, restrain harmful arrogance, heal wounded souls, shape personal decisions, interrupt destructive habits, stimulate spiritual growth, and transform lives. God reshapes the human soul through worship.

Since ancient times, people have gathered to seek God through prayer, story, music, song, fellowship, and mutual compassion. *Synagogue* means "to bring together." God lives in the people gathered in devotion and covenant. And the Latin word *ecclesia*, the root of our word for church, means "called out of the world." God calls us out of the ordinary life of work, family, and leisure into the presence of the sacred so that we can develop the spiritual resources that guide and sustain fruitful living.

Worship is the reason God liberated the Hebrew people from the oppressions of slavery. God spoke to Moses, saying, "Release my people so they can worship me" (Exodus 8:1, *The Message*). God desires our devotion.

Jesus presents the highest of God's desires this way, "That you love the Lord your God with all your passion and prayer and muscle and intelligence—and that you love your neighbor as well as you do yourself" (Luke 10:27, *The Message*). Heart, mind, soul, and strength—in worship we offer all to God in love.

Worship provides the most likely setting for the change of heart and mind we describe as *justification*, the moment of conscious awareness and decision that involves our receiving God's grace through Christ, confessing our need for God, accepting God's pardon, and turning our lives toward God and away from former ways. Jesus tells the story of the Pharisee and the tax collector entering the Temple (Luke 18:9-14). The Pharisee is so full of himself that he is unable to open himself to God. The tax collector, consciously aware of his brokenness and spiritual emptiness, genuinely offers his heart to God. Jesus says the tax collector leaves a different person than when he came in. He is *justified*—by grace his life freshly aligns with God. He discovers a new relationship with God through open-hearted worship and devotion to God.

In the Gospels, Jesus and his followers regularly attend temple, read from Scripture, speak of giving, practice prayer, retreat to God, give thanks, and observe the sabbath. Worship becomes their natural breath. Worship strengthens them for ministry. Living in God involves returning God's love.

Read Luke 18:9-14.

When has a worship experience changed your heart and mind and provided you with fresh spiritual insights? When do you feel closest to God in worship?

Prayer: Lord, cause me to be what you have called me to be: shaped by your Spirit and changed by my love for Christ. Make me right with you; align me with your love.

13

Day Thirteen

" 'You shall love the Lord your God with all your heart, and with all your soul, and with all your mind.' This is the greatest and first commandment." —Matthew 22:37-38

What happens in worship, and why is it important?

First, worship connects us to God and to other people who love God. If God's unconditional love is the pivotal truth of life, how and why do we set aside time to focus on God, to receive God's love, and to love God in return? God desires a relationship with us, and in response to God's seeking us, worship is our way of seeking God, our reaching upward to God's reaching downward.

Second, worship helps us to discover the transcendent, spiritual aspects of life. Human beings are not oriented merely by one sense or two, but by many. Imagine a room full of people; one third understand and speak only German, another third only Spanish, and another third only English. If we speak only one language, we leave two-thirds of the people unaddressed. If we want to communicate with all of them, we will have to learn other languages.

Likewise with the interior life: perhaps only one third of the knowledge and wisdom to live meaningfully is reducible to and reachable by conscious, linear, rational thought. This we learn through words, sermons, and the sharing of ideas. But another third of insight and experience that expands our sense of meaning, motivation, and connection comes to us through music, silence, movement, liturgy, and a host of other means. These are truths we absorb in ways beyond our conscious awareness. Nevertheless, they form us, strengthen us, and connect us to God and one another. And another third of insight and truth comes through the experience of being together with others, our sense of belonging. Worship grants us a coherent sense of belonging, of purpose, and of future. Practicing worship is like learning other languages that open us to the full resources of the spiritual life. God's transcendent love pulls us out of ourselves, stretches us, and takes us beyond where we could possibly arrive on our own.

Third, worship puts us in the most advantageous place for engaging the Spirit. While God is present in all of life, it is through worship that we purposefully search for God and become acutely aware of God's presence. We give our attention to God and listen for God with greater intentionality. Worship represents a regular appointment with the sacred, a planned encounter, a scheduled time and place to connect. We arrive with souls prepared, minds ready, and hearts open; and our anticipation makes worship different from other times.

Fourth, worship brings us back to ourselves, grounding us in what really matters. People frequently describe worship as the activity during their week that centers or anchors them, revealing the risk we feel of losing touch, becoming distracted, and disconnected, or living haphazard and harried lives rather than feeling rooted in what really matters. Worship carves out a time to focus on the larger questions of life; it lifts our eyes beyond the immediate and tangible to look at life from a wider perspective. We have time to reflect, anticipate, reprioritize, and to push the reset button in our spiritual lives when we might otherwise veer off course from our most vital relationships. Worship provides a way by which we let ourselves be found, a way to find God, and to find ourselves.

The purpose of worship does not begin and end with what human beings do; worship is the means God uses to accomplish God's purposes in the human heart and in the community of Christ. In worship, God offers a setting for us to confess our brokenness, receive pardon, and relieve our guilt. Worship itself, and every element of it, is a means of grace, a way for God to accomplish our re-creation.

Read Matthew 22:34-40.

What replenishes your spirit and refreshes you in worship? How does God use worship to speak to you? How do worship, prayer, and music change you?

Prayer: Dear God, may I always be eager to offer you my very best. Let my worship be authentic, alive, and marked with a passionate longing for you.

14

Day Fourteen

"Make a joyful noise to the LORD, all the earth.
Worship the LORD with gladness;
come into his presence with singing."
—Psalm 100:1-2

Any attempt to completely describe worship falls short. In ways we cannot fully comprehend, we practice visible and tangible behaviors which result in our feeling sustained, forgiven, connected, motivated to make better choices, and called to serve others. How that happens often remains beyond conscious awareness. Worship is mystery.

Why does repeating the history of God's grace, praying, giving God thanks, kneeling with others, and receiving a piece of bread and a taste of grape juice affect us? I have received the sacrament of Holy Communion and presided over its liturgy thousands of times, and yet I feel utterly inadequate explaining why and how participating in this simple ritual affects the human spirit. The bread itself does not change its substance, and afterward remains merely bread as beforehand. But through our remembering Christ and his conscious commitment to the salvation of the world and by inviting the Spirit's presence, we change the use of these ordinary elements. We're taking Christ into us as God is taking us into the body of Christ. By repeating the sacrament, the practice has a mysteriously formative impact on our lives. Something below the surface goes on, something real and life-changing.

While receiving the broken bread in his hands, Carl felt struck by the reconciling sacrifice of Christ. He thought about his brother with whom he had not spoken for more than five years, and the brokenness he sensed. In an unexpected moment of clarity, he realized how much responsibility he himself carried for the disconnection. "Life is too short, and someone has to take the first step," he thought. That afternoon, he phoned his brother and began a conversation. By reconnecting to his brother, Carl filled a part of himself that was empty.

Communion is not merely a *confirming* sacrament that reassures us of our belonging to the community of Christ; it is a *converting* sacrament God uses to reframe our hearts and redirect our behaviors. The regular repeating of the sacrament creates us anew.

Likewise with other sacraments and services, their effect and meaning are both mysterious and real. God loves us even before we represent God's grace with the sacrament of baptism; we belong to the body of Christ even without the membership pledge that makes our intentions known. But in our saying and doing these things, deep invisible hopes and graces become tangible, visible, and public. Mysteriously, our rituals connect us to God.

Music is another aspect of worship that connects us with God. It is a mystery how music shapes the human spirit, but it does. Music helps us say things we have trouble speaking in words. Singing lifts us out of ourselves and binds us together. Music is a principal means by which we explore, discover, and receive spirituality.

Music takes us on a trip to the other side of our brains where fact, data, rationality, and objectivity end like a pier extending over a sea with unfathomable depths.

Perhaps the greatest mystery involves how the affectionate attention to ordinary things in worship—prayer, music, liturgy, Scripture, sacrament, offering, fellowship—reveals a beauty, meaning, and coherence that opens us to the discovery and rediscovery of grace in everyday situations. Worship trains our attentiveness to God, attunes us to noticing the Spirit. Our quality of attention to God improves; and we begin to see God's work, sense God's presence, and discern God's call more naturally. One hour each week changes all the other hours of our week.

Worship is mystery, and part of our task is not merely to wrestle with the mystery or seek to avoid it, but to embrace it and receive it.

Read 1 Corinthians 11:23-26.

Have you felt your spirit lifted to God by music? How does singing shape your spiritual life? What about the sacrament of Holy Communion refreshes you or sustains you?

Prayer: Open the eyes of my heart, Lord, so that I may see your extraordinary presence among us in our ordinary worship each week. Help me remember you, and discover you, in each prayer and song and sermon and sacrament.

15

Day Fifteen

[Jesus] said to them, "Come away to a deserted place all by yourselves and rest a while." —Mark 6:31

Daily personal prayer and devotion deepen our relationship with God and prepare us for community worship. People who practice loving God in return carve out time in each day to intentionally focus on God, to express gratitude, offer private confession, and lift petitions and intercessions. Prayer at fixed times, such as morning prayers when rising, grace before meals, or evening prayers at the close of the day help us create a space in our lives for God. Daily habit provides the same restorative, centering, and encouraging quality to daily life that community worship adds to weekly life. Short devotional reading, reciting a prayer, or the simple observance of silence settles us in God. We orient ourselves a little each day toward God. Daily prayer blesses us.

We can't develop a meaningful relationship with someone if we don't spend time with them. The same is true with our relationship with God. Daily prayer and private worship is time with God.

Frequently, we cling too tightly to anger, blame, hate, hurt, grief, guilt, and sadness. How can we restore our souls, heal our brokenness, and relieve our fear? Daily prayer filters our experiences through our relationship with God. Through patterns of personal devotion, we perceive life differently, regulate negative emotions, and lift them up to God. One kind of experience becomes something else entirely through prayer as we move toward transformation, resurrection, and a continuing rebirth. Prayer gives us courage to choose paths that lead to life.

Personal prayer changes our relationships with friends, coworkers, strangers, and even those toward whom we feel animosity. The places in ourselves that are most disconnected from God, when explored persistently and honestly in prayer, lead us also to reconciliation with others. We repair disconnection with others through soul work; inner peace reaps an outward harvest.

Daily personal devotion prepares us for community worship. God's ability to reach us increases as we cooperate with the Holy Spirit in making ready our souls to receive God's word. Personal prayer fosters eagerness for community worship.

People who practice loving God in return carry their daily lives with them into prayer and worship, and carry worship and prayer with them into their daily lives. They live so that their whole life glorifies and praises God.

They cultivate the gifts of silence and waiting. Clarity is born in spiritual stillness. They create times to pause, rest, listen, and prepare themselves for God. As for all the practices, a pattern of Passionate Worship requires a surrendering, a yielding of ourselves and of our will, a giving up of some good things in order to attend to greater things. Surrender involves trust, openness, and vulnerability. Following Christ involves an incremental relinquishing of our control in order to allow God's Spirit to form us anew. To "have in us the mind that is in Christ" is a gradual process, a maturing, a becoming. There are no experts, only learners, and those who have stepped down the path a little farther than we have. We gradually feel less awkward, more connected, more confident in the face of the resistances, and immeasurably more aware of the blessings that accrue with falling in love with God.

We worship because we love God. We do it to connect to other people. We do it to find ourselves. Worship fosters joy, connection, self-understanding, and meaning. Worship fundamentally changes us.

Read Matthew 6:25-33.

How do your daily prayers help you connect to God? How does praying with others help you sense God's Spirit at work?

Prayer: Help me remember, dear God, that in returning to you, I find strength; in resting in you, I find peace; and in trusting you, I find quietness.

16

Day Sixteen

"But what happens when we live God's way? He brings gifts into our lives, much the same way that fruit appears in an orchard— things like affection for others, exuberance about life, serenity."
—*Galatians 5:22*, The Message

Helen grew up active in the Christian faith. At her baptism as an infant, her parents vowed to support her growth in grace. As a child, Helen learned songs in vacation Bible school, led youth services, and worshipped outdoors at summer camp. At confirmation, she committed herself to follow Christ. At her wedding, she and her husband made public their covenant before God. Helen adapted patterns of worship with each phase of her life, shaped by her own changing needs.

She became one of those people to whom others instinctively turn for insight and counsel. She wore the mantel of spiritual encourager with great humility. She was even-tempered, warm, open, and gracious.

Helen's rich interior life overflowed into the lives of others. Her soul work helped others with theirs. She invited people into the life of the church, making room for strangers, becoming a friend and encourager.

Helen was diagnosed with cancer when she was in her mid-fifties. For two years she faced the uncertain and anguishing rhythm of progress and setback. All those people she had loved came back into her own life as caregivers and prayer partners. She grew weaker physically, but continued to strengthen everyone around. People found themselves overwhelmed by her sense of peace and the ease by which she accepted death itself as a kind of grace. Her funeral was a celebration of life, an expression of gratitude to God for a life well-lived.

Helen was deep-hearted, generous, grounded, and wise. She became that kind of person through a lifetime of worship.

Imagine if we could extract from Helen's life all the formative worship experiences that impacted her. Imagine if we could remove the tens of thousands of hymns, sermons, and prayers. Imagine if we could take away the baptismal vows taken by her parents, the covenant she embraced at her wedding, all the daily morning prayers she offered, the prayers she taught at the bedside of her children. After extracting all these experiences, who would she be?

We would not recognize her as the same person. The lifelong practice of loving God fundamentally changed her. In worship, she made the most critical decisions and commitments of her life. Through worship, she became someone she otherwise never would have become.

Those who practice Passionate Worship attend worship frequently and consistently until it becomes a valued and sustaining pattern for them. They love worship because they love God.

They enter worship with hearts and minds prepared. They eagerly anticipate how God may connect to them. They pray for the pastor, the musicians, and all who lead worship. They ask themselves, "What is God saying to me today through the songs, the Scripture and sermon, the sacrament, or the fellowship of others?" Loving God means listening for God.

People who practice Passionate Worship let music into their souls. They lift their voices in praise to God. They let themselves sing.

They love God, and they invest themselves wholeheartedly in cultivating their relationship with God. They let God reach them and change them through worship. They foster the spiritual life.

God uses worship to reach us, to change our hearts, and to make us God's own. Through worship, we reach for God in return, devoting ourselves with passion so that we begin to see the world through God's eyes. God loves us, and God uses our practice of loving God in return to form us into followers of Jesus Christ.

"I am the vine," Jesus said, "you are the branches" (John 15:5). Worship connects the branches to the vine, keeps us connected to the source of life, and helps us grow in Christ.

Read Isaiah 40:28-31.

How has God shaped you through your worship and prayer? How have you made worship a priority? How does your love for God strengthen you?

Prayer: By your Spirit, make us one with Christ, one with each other, and one in ministry to all the world.

Growing in Grace

THE PRACTICE OF
INTENTIONAL FAITH DEVELOPMENT

The practice of *Intentional Faith Development* involves purposefully learning in community outside of worship in order to deepen our faith and to grow in grace and in the knowledge and love of God. Through Bible studies, classes, retreats, or other small-group ministries, we do the soul work that connects us to others, immerses us in God's Word, and fosters our growth in grace.

Intentional means having a plan in mind. It derives from the Latin word which means *to stretch out for*, *to aim at*. Just as through consistent physical exercise or committed practice on a musical instrument, things that are currently impossible become possible, intentionality in our spiritual lives helps us become a different kind of person. We learn Christ.

During the days to come, we focus on how God uses our experiences in Christian community to reach into our lives to work for our well-being. Reflect on your relationship to God, and where you are today in terms of following Christ. If you continue on the same trajectory, how will your relationship with God and your following of Christ be different five years from now?

Teach me to do your will, for you are my God.
Change me from the inside out.

17

Day Seventeen

"Let us consider how to provoke one another to love and good deeds, not neglecting to meet together, as is the habit of some, but encouraging one another . . ." —Hebrews 10:24-25

Rita and Joel teach an eight-week Bible study focused on the parables of Jesus. Six years before, they began their own journey into the exploration of Scripture. They'd been active in the congregation for several months when they responded to an invitation to a series on Philippians. The study stoked their curiosity. The next year, they joined a Disciple Bible study, an in-depth, long-term study. "Belonging to that Bible study was one of the best things we ever did. We began to feel comfortable with the Bible and to feel at home with other people in the congregation."

When they continued to participate in Bible studies, they were surprised and humbled when the pastor asked if they would teach a class themselves. The pastor assured them that their task involved facilitating the discussion, helping participants learn from one another, and learning to explore Scripture together. They attended a two-hour training, and then agreed to teach the class.

An interesting mix of people signed up for their Bible study: a thirty-something, new-to-the-church accountant comes with her friend who lives in her apartment complex; a physician and his wife who works at home with Mom duties; a woman who works as a bank vice-president; a younger couple who are both teachers; another dual-career couple with technology backgrounds; and a recently divorced man employed at a sporting goods store.

With everything ready, folks begin to gather, welcoming one another, catching up, getting their snacks, finding their places. An air of comfort has emerged after only a few weeks together and there are handshakes and embraces and good-humored bantering.

Rita opens the meeting with prayer and introduces the three parables they will explore from Luke 15. Some have read the Scriptures and the workbook thoroughly, and others have spent less time in preparation, but everyone expresses initial reactions to what they have read. They share easily. A sense of compassion, an atmosphere of winsomeness, a willingness to listen, and a mysterious and natural intimacy make this time together different from other gatherings, such as staff meetings at work or classrooms at college.

As the evening ends, Joel leads in prayer as people lift concerns. Afterward, people continue visiting with one another as they leave.

This scenario describes a typical Bible study that includes some of the key elements that mark a wide variety of small-group gatherings—a focus on faith and Scripture, a sense of community, the sharing of prayer. Some meet on Sunday mornings and others on weekday nights; some studies last six weeks and others continue for decades; some are formal, structured, and driven by lessons and resources while others are freestyle and unstructured. Growing together in Christ takes many forms.

Faith development refers to how we purposefully *learn in community* outside of worship in order to deepen our faith and to grow in grace and in the knowledge and love of God. Faith development also takes place through retreats, camping ministries, seminars, and support groups that apply faithful living to particular contexts and challenges such as parenting, divorce recovery, living with Alzheimer's, and countless other topics. All of these ministries embed us in a community that helps us to mature in faith and to follow Christ more nearly in our daily living.

Read Psalm 1:1-3.

When have you belonged to a Bible study or class that was helpful, sustaining, and spiritually satisfying?

Prayer: Your hands have made and fashioned me, O Lord. Thank you for deep-spirited friends and for all those people you send to me to share my journey to you.

18

Day Eighteen

"For where two or three are gathered in my name, I am there among them."
—Matthew 18:20

We learn in community because Jesus taught us to learn this way. He weaved people into a community around him and taught them through stories, parables, examples, and by modeling the life of grace. The practice of learning in community continued during the beginnings of the early church. The second chapter of Acts reports people gathering in home and temple to learn from the disciples. The community provided a supportive network for testing ideas, gaining from other people's experiences, sharing the love of Christ, and holding one another accountable to following Christ.

John Wesley, founder of Methodism, intentionally organized people into small groups for the study of Scripture, prayer, and to "watch after one another in love."[5] Early Methodists gathered in homes and workplaces and schools. They inquired after one another's spiritual progress with a supportive intimacy. They shared their doubts and hopes and talked about how they had seen God's grace at work in their lives. They encouraged one another.

Theologically, Wesley based the class meetings on the sanctifying grace of God. *Sanctification* involves our growing in faith and how the Holy Spirit works within us to help us mature in Christ. By the grace of God, we pray that we are closer to God and further along in our following of Christ now than we were five years ago. And we pray that we will be closer to God and further along in our walk with Christ five years from now than we are today.

Sanctification means our faith journey has direction, trajectory, purpose, a path. We desire to become more Christ-like. We grow in grace and in the knowledge and love of God.

According to Wesley, the Holy Spirit makes this maturation process possible. However, growth in Christ requires us to *cooperate* with the Holy Spirit in our own sanctification. We cooperate by placing ourselves in the most advantageous situations for learning God's heart, for walking in Jesus' way, and for remaining faithful in our practice of the spiritual life. A congregation or a community of Christ, such as a Bible study, class, or support group, becomes a "school for love" as we learn to give and receive love, to serve others, and to follow Christ more nearly. Community provides the catalyst for growth in Christ.

Peace, forgiveness, mercy, compassion, hope, gentleness, love, grace, serving—these and many other components of belief and practice are communal in nature. They are social and cannot be learned merely from a book. They become part of us as we practice them with other people.

When we share the journey with other people, they keep us committed just as we keep them on the path of growth in Christ. Practices are best honed with the help of others. Those who share our journey comfort us, provoke us, remind us, sympathize with us, confront us, and pray for us. The Holy Spirit uses them to draw us further along toward Christ.

It is in community that we discover Christ. Wesley wrote, "Christianity is essentially a social religion; and . . . to turn it into a solitary one is to destroy it."[6] An entirely solitary religion is an impossible contradiction in the following of Christ.

Read Acts 2:37-47.

How do you tend to your spiritual growth? How have other people served as a catalyst for your own spiritual growth?

Prayer: Focus my heart on things true, noble, authentic, compelling, and gracious—the best, not the worst; the life-giving rather than the life-sapping. Build me up in you.

Day Nineteen

". . . straining forward to what lies ahead, I press on toward the goal
for the prize of the heavenly call of God in Christ Jesus."
—Philippians 3:13-14

How do you find time for Bible study? One young professional woman answered, "By prearrangement with myself. I manage to do other things on time—go to the gym, take children to school and to soccer practice, eat, work. I look at my Bible study as a support group, a regular appointment with God's grace. I make it a priority, as if keeping an appointment with Jesus."

Many followers of Christ desire and value small-group experiences and have benefited from them in the past, but their participation is haphazard, incidental, and infrequent. A short-term study piques their interest at one point and a few years later they attend a home Bible study. Years pass before they go with friends on a weekend retreat. The pattern lacks thoroughness, frequency, and focus. They never practice with enough depth and consistency to feel comfortable or confident with their spirituality. They dabble in religion without growing in grace. Scripture remains strange, mysterious, impenetrable. They enjoy the fellowship but never appreciate close, long-term bonds that lend a sense of trust, strength, and depth to their relationships with others in the community.

Intentional means having a plan in mind. It refers to our determination to act in a specific manner and our having a purpose to what we do. *Intentional* means *to stretch out for, to aim at.* Paul describes this yearning for greater fullness when he writes, "straining forward to what lies ahead, I press on toward the goal for the prize of the heavenly call of God in Christ Jesus" (Philippians 3:13-14). We seek the perfect love of Christ, to have in us the mind that was in Christ Jesus.

Intentional ratchets up the commitment and consistency. Those who practice Intentional Faith Development make room in their lives for learning faith. They *plan* to feed their spirits. Learning faith becomes a way of life, a practice that is no longer haphazard and incidental but which is central and important. They *regularly* participate in Bible studies, seminars, or retreats to focus on cultivating the spiritual life. They desire to know God, and set themselves to the task of learning God's word through Scripture. Learning becomes a lifelong priority, and they seek progressively more challenging experiences to deepen their understanding of God. They feed their curiosity. They desire to mature in Christ and put themselves in the most advantageous situations to do so. Priority, purpose, consistency, persistence, and commitment make faith development *intentional.*

The practice of Intentional Faith Development refers to our purposeful learning in Christian community in order to grow in grace and in the knowledge and love of God.

Read Matthew 7:7-14.

What keeps you aware of the spiritual dimension in your daily life? What are you curious about in the spiritual life, and how do you explore faith more deeply?

Prayer: Cultivate in me a life of wonder, faith, love, steadiness, and service. The life to which you call me, may I embrace it fervently and forever.

20

Day Twenty

"All scripture is inspired by God and is useful for teaching, for reproof, for correction, and for training in righteousness." —2 Timothy 3:16

Focus on Scripture has the effect of pulling each person out of his or her immediate situation to give a larger view, a slightly more universal perspective. Amazingly, people from vastly different circumstances can read a parable prayerfully, or hear someone share a personal experience about God's activity, and each feels that the topic strikes the target to address a particular challenge in his or her own life.

The benefit of sifting through Scripture with companions cannot be reduced to gleaning helpful hints for living or from the advice our friends give us. Each person learns something relevant to his or her soul's desire. As meaning is unlocked by one person on a topic, an overflowing of insight connects to other persons.

And by the grace of God, with frequent and consistent participation in the faith community, various spiritually sustaining attributes are deepened; people find themselves with more courage, more patience, a greater compassion, more resolve, more peace. Like a potter forming clay, God gently and persistently shapes us.

Knowing God, with time, mysteriously causes us to become a different kind of person, with more depth, peace, and courage. We become more hopeful, more thankful, less reactive, gentler, more patient, more resilient, less angry, better able to relate. Whether these transformations are slow or fast, unrevealed or dramatic—knowing God changes us from the inside out. We follow Christ more closely. We are born afresh.

Focused learning also heightens our spiritual awareness. It opens the spiritual world to us and stimulates an attentiveness that helps us see elements of soul and grace we might never have noticed before. God awakens us to new life.

Some years ago, I spotted what I thought was an unusually beautiful and rare bird near my home. After searching bird guide books, I discovered that the strikingly colorful bird was actually quite common in my area. After I saw it once, I began to see it regularly. I wondered what else I was missing. With a new intentionality, I began to read about birds and talk with birders. I learned where and how to look, I learned their habits. Prior to my "conversion," seeing birds was accidental and unintentional for me; I had little appreciation for them. With intentionality, I began to see the world around me from a different perspective.

In the same way, when we open Scripture, belong to a community of Christ, and start to explore life with God, we detect God's presence and activity that we never before noticed. A new world opens. We learn a new vocabulary. With soul work, an unseen world that we never knew existed becomes visible. Regular Bible study with others brings topics before us that we otherwise overlook, and we learn to identify them with greater clarity. We learn to see God.

Jesus came to open the eyes of the blind (Luke 4:18). As we delve into Scripture, we look afresh at our family life, our work world, our inner life, and the world around us. When we notice how the Spirit moves, we perceive signs of grace. Hope, joy, forgiveness, service, spirit, grace—these and other elements of faith become visible and tangible.

Without intentionally cultivating faith, we go through life self-blinded, seeing only a portion of what is before us. We perceive the world through cultural filters that make it nearly impossible to see what is really most important. Learning in community opens our eyes.

Read John 3:1-17.

What keeps you aware of the spiritual dimension in your daily life? How have you learned to see God in fresh ways?

Prayer: Heal me from dimness of sight; awaken me from dullness of spirit. Lord, make me alive. Teach me the usefulness of your Word—showing me life-truths, exposing my rebellion, correcting my misjudgments, and training me in Jesus' way.

21

Day Twenty-One

[Jesus] said to him, "Do you want to be made well?" —John 5:6

Belonging to a learning faith community provides companionship that sustains us through difficult experiences. Nothing is as disheartening as a lonely struggle. Many communities and congregations are too large for people to know others well, and so it's in the intimacy of small groups—classes, Bible studies, choirs, prayer groups—that we pray for one another and learn to care for one another.

As we pray for one another, we feel hopeful, connected. And that makes all the difference during times of doubt, suffering, or loss. Communion with one another deepens our communion to God.

The thread of life is fragile. A few cells within a healthy body grow erratically and we receive the diagnosis of cancer; a second's misjudgment at an intersection, and a life is lost; a heart that keeps its cadence for decades skips a few beats and we find ourselves in intensive care; a friend loses her baby during pregnancy; an aging parent shows signs of Alzheimer's; violence strikes someone we know. None of us is immune to such devastating experiences.

We overestimate our capacity to handle these things all by ourselves, and we underestimate the power of community to help. Belonging to a caring community, we discover a sustenance that does not answer all our questions, but which keeps us connected, rooted, grounded. When the worst happens, God doesn't promise us an answer; God provides us a relationship. Through sustaining relationships, we discover that God is not aloof from life and disinterested in us. Instead, God gets in the trenches and suffers with us. God's presence reaches us through the people who love us. The thread of life is fragile, but the fabric of life is eternal.

Belonging to a supportive community provides an interpretive context that helps us understand our experience with greater clarity and hopefulness. Stories from Scripture, mutual prayer, and receiving the embrace of others help us move from one place in our soul to another, from despair to hope, from death to life.

By ourselves, any one of the challenges that beset us can paralyze us. Community pulls us out of ourselves and carries us toward God.

I remember visiting a woman whose husband had died a few months before. She sat in her rocking chair in her living room from morning to evening. In front of her rested the urn that contained her husband's ashes. Every day was spent sitting in her chair focusing on her loss. With continued contact, her friends and I began to reconnect her to her community, and she became part of a women's Bible study. Some months later, I visited again. The rocking chair now faced a window with a phone beside it. Letters she was addressing for a church project were scattered on the table. The urn rested on a shelf above the fireplace, still present but no longer the focal point of her existence.

This example has become symbolic for me. Jesus confronted the person paralyzed beside the pool for thirty-eight years with the question, "Do you want to be made well?" (John 5:6). In the gloom of grief, depression, loss, and pain, the answer is not simple. Belonging to a faith community helps us to enfold our past into the present and future, to integrate suffering into a coherent understanding of who we are today and what God intends for our future.

People who practice Intentional Faith Development commit themselves to learning the faith and growing in grace. They overcome excuses, make time, find a learning community, and commit to it. They delve deeper.

They find a way to learn that fits their own temperament and learning style. They experiment and explore until something works that sustains their spiritual curiosity and growth in Christ. They learn how to learn.

Read John 5:1-9.

When was a time you helped sustain another person during a time of difficulty or grief? When have you felt sustained? How does God's love heal us?

Prayer: Save me, Lord, from my own arrogant sense of self-sufficiency. Open me to love others and be loved by others.

22

Day Twenty-Two

"For just as the body is one and has many members, and all the members of the body, though many, are one body, so it is with Christ." —1 Corinthians 12:12

Tammy said, "Each time I leave a Bible study session, I feel encouraged to do things I was fearful to do before. We always end up talking each other into things—to speak up at work, to forgive a sister, to visit someone who is grieving. We know these are the right things to do. But we need a nudge." Community fosters accountability. We become the voice of Christ to each other.

God uses community to save us from ourselves and the self-destructive choices we make. When we face temptations beyond what we can bear, our friends in Christ reinforce our resolve, strengthen our covenants, and remind us of the critical commitments that bind us.

A thin spirituality that is untested and uncorrected by community leads to self-deception; in honest community, we recognize our incredible capacity to delude ourselves. Jesus says, "Where two or three or gathered in my name, I am there among them" (Matthew 18:20). Christ's voice, in our sisters and brothers, brings us back to ourselves, sustains us, and heals us. In the gift of community we discover the power of confession and of forgiveness.

In community we also find spiritual encouragement. There, we catch the contagious quality of faith and hope. To *encourage* literally means *to put courage into, to give heart*! We become more in Christ because of the influence of friends. We talk one another into things. We take bolder action that we might otherwise avoid. We follow Christ more eagerly. Like Tammy said, we sometimes need the nudge.

It is also in community that we practice caring for one another. In the love others show us, we catch a partial and imperfect glimpse of the complete and unconditional love God has for us. Our burdens are not ours to bear entirely on our own. By sharing Christ, we share life.

Growth results not merely from what we do, but most especially from *what God does*. Opening ourselves to Scripture, praying for one another, and caring for one another are concrete and personal ways God reaches into our lives to work for our well-being. Our participation invites the Holy Spirit to cooperate with us in the perfecting of our love. Talking and praying and laughing and learning create a dynamic that lifts Jesus' teachings off the page and puts them into daily practice. The Bible comes alive, a letter from God, the source of assurance, belonging, and invitation. God works through community.

God has hard-wired us for belonging; learning how to give and receive love is an essential element of human existence and the key to flourishing. Jesus said, "I am the vine, you are the branches" (John 15:5). As we stay connected to Christ, we thrive; disconnected, we wither. Community is God's way of bringing us Christ.

People who practice Intentional Faith Development avail themselves of increasingly more challenging learning opportunities. They ask themselves, "What am I learning now that is different from an earlier age?" They stretch.

They avoid the temptation to make scriptural exploration abstract and detached from life. They ask, "What is God reminding me of in this message? What is God inviting me to do?" They connect God to life.

People who grow in grace realize that if they follow Christ for a thousand years, they will still need to learn as much on the last day as on the first. The sanctifying grace of God never ends. In each season they recommit to some form of study or class or retreat. They open themselves anew to insight and community. They become resilient, malleable, and adaptable rather than fixed, stagnant, and impenetrable. They rekindle the love of God within themselves at every step and stage of life. They cultivate the spiritual life.

Read Romans 12:1-18.

When have you been encouraged by friends in a faith community to follow Christ more closely, eagerly, or boldly?

Prayer: By your Spirit, weave me into the fabric of faith, build me into the body of Christ, create in me a sense of belonging and connection to you through other people.

Loving and Serving Others

THE PRACTICE OF RISK-TAKING MISSION AND SERVICE

The practice of *Risk-Taking Mission and Service* involves offering ourselves in purposeful service and making a positive difference, even at significant personal cost and inconvenience to our own lives.

Mission and Service involves our deliberate effort to relieve suffering; confront injustice; and assist during times of crisis, loss, or grief. *Mission and Service* connects us with people we don't know. Our following Christ transforms the world around us.

Risk-Taking Mission and Service pushes us out of our comfort zone and into places we would never go on our own. Those who practice such service go where Jesus leads, even when it is uncomfortable, awkward, unexpected, and costly. They risk.

During the next several days, pray for those who work on the front lines of service—the people who feed the hungry, give shelter to the homeless, heal the sick, visit the imprisoned, and reach out to the lonely and poor. Pray for a discerning mind and open heart to see how God may be calling you to transform the part of the world and the piece of Christ's mission given to you.

Thank you, Christ, for inviting me to serve in your name, to give life and receive life in loving others as you love them.

23

Day Twenty-Three

Then Jesus went to work on his disciples. . . . "Don't run from suffering;
embrace it. Follow me and I'll show you how. Self-help is no help at all. Self-
sacrifice is the way, my way, to finding yourself, your true self."
—*Matthew 16:24-25*, The Message

We live to ourselves. It is comfortable, safe, and natural to do so. Each of us has a whole world of private concerns, personal passions, hobbies, entertainments, family responsibilities, and work obligations. The circle in which we live, work, and play is small, but intense, and important. And it is ours. Why give the time or make the effort to reach beyond our world to serve other people? And would it make any real difference, anyway?

"Most people, given the choice between having a better world, or a better place within the world as it is, would choose the latter." This cynical analysis of the human condition, attributed to Ralph W. Sockman, captures the magnitude of the issue. Our energy naturally goes to making a better place for ourselves. Society convinces us that this is the best way to care for ourselves and our families.

So, why serve others? Why work for a better world?

First, some people serve others out of a sense of duty, obligation, and responsibility. Helping others is imperative, and they serve others without regard to the personal cost or inconvenience. Imagine how it would change your life to take Jesus' commands seriously, and to cultivate such trust that when Jesus says "do it," you would respond with complete and utter obedience.

Second, there are those who serve because helping others contributes to the social fabric of human life. Living in this world requires an unspoken social contract that requires me to help you when you need it, trusting that you will help me when I need it. Serving greases the machinery of social interaction and creates a sustainable mutuality that is essential for co-existence.

Third, some people discover that serving provides immeasurable personal satisfaction for themselves. They like the way it feels to know that the work they have done, a project they have sponsored, or a policy they have supported has truly relieved suffering, or improved the conditions of people in need. As one person says, "I like myself better and I'm happier when I help others in concrete ways." Making a difference enriches our lives, adds an element of enchantment and adventure and satisfaction that other activities cannot match.

The Holy Spirit purifies all of these motivations when we serve others with the right spirit and focus genuinely on meeting human needs in ways that respect recipients and serve the purposes of Christ.

Need-focused service and passion-driven commitment do not necessarily conflict. In *Wishful Thinking*, Frederick Buechner describes God's call to service and ministry as "the place where your deep gladness and the world's deep hunger meet."[7]

Picture a graph-like matrix. Along the left side of the graph are all the deep human needs, sufferings, and challenges that require bold and courageous service. These are the things God needs people to work on. Along the bottom of the graph are all the particular gifts and passions that characterize our life. These things personally motivate us. Somewhere on the graph, unmet needs intersect with our own personal passions, and that's where we find ourselves offering effective help. That's where we take our place in God's service, making a difference in ways we find satisfying.

Read Luke 10:25-37.

What particular gifts, abilities, or experiences prepare you to make a positive difference personally or in your community? Where do the world's unmet needs intersect with your own personal passion?

Prayer: Give me an obedient heart, Lord, to do those things I know you call me to do but which I nevertheless neglect or ignore. Forgive me. Change me. Use me.

24
Day Twenty-Four

"For those who want to save their life will lose it, and those who lose their life for my sake, and for the sake of the gospel, will save it."
—Mark 8:35

Philosophers ponder the question of why a stranger walking by a burning building and hearing the cry of someone inside would put his life at risk to enter the building to try to save a person he does not know.

The stranger who responds puts everything on the line in that moment. He places at risk his entire future—seeing his children graduate and grow to adulthood, decades of support for his family, years of affectionate partnership with his wife, all that he might accomplish for the remainder of his natural life. In a split-second decision to enter the burning building, he puts all this at risk for a person he does not know and without regard as to whether the person deserves it or not, is healthy or sick, is rich or poor. Why does he do it? Is he out of touch with reality?

In that critical moment of pure insight and absolute choice, the person *is not out of touch with reality*. In that moment the person *perceives the truest reality* of all, that our lives are interconnected, that our futures are intertwined with one another, and that we are ultimately one. In moments of such revelation, we see so clearly that we are propelled to the highest and truest of responses. If I let you die, I kill something inside myself.

Ultimately people are not isolated egos, separate and self-absorbed, capable only of self-preservation. I do not live in a universe occupied only by myself. We are one; we belong to one body. In theological terms, you belong to me and I belong to you because we both belong to God. You are my sister or brother and I am yours because God gives both of us life and loves us both unconditionally and completely. God's grace laces our lives inextricably together. When I perceive that reality, I can do no other than to try to help you.

In the bold, risky, sacrificial action of entering a burning building to aid a stranger, we witness a raw distillation of the impulses toward what is true. We willingly pour ourselves out because no other way ultimately leads to life.

The deeper truth that we see so clearly in dramatic life-and-death events is one we intuitively perceive in our daily lives and non-critical moments, and this leads us to pour out our lives in small ways each day in service to our families, our children, our communities, and even to strangers. A well-lived life that is in touch with reality involves sacrificing ourselves in the daily care of our children, the love of a spouse, the care of a neighbor, and the service to strangers, each day giving parts of ourselves up, and losing our lives for others. Nothing sustains the flourishing of life and spirit like genuinely pouring ourselves into the lives of others. This does not diminish life; it fulfills it. This is love.

On September 11, 2001, the United States experienced unfathomable pain and loss with the deaths of innocent people. In the countless heroic stories of people who sacrificed their lives to save others, the world also perceived a glimpse of the reality of human connection that was sharper and more focused than we usually see. The tragedy provoked a reality check for countless people, causing them to explore profound questions, such as "Who am I? Who is important to me? How am I related to the people around me? What really matters?" In the brokenness, violence, and grief, we also saw more clearly than usual what is sustaining and trustworthy.

Read Matthew 25:31-40.

Where have you seen God working in the midst of loss and suffering? How have you been a part of God's work? What are some small ways you pour out your life to others each day?

Prayer: Help me forget myself enough to truly help others. Shape my worries into prayers and my prayers into practices that serve your purposes as I serve others.

25

Day Twenty-Five

*"Whoever wants to be great must become a servant. . . . That is what the
Son of Man has done: He came to serve, not be served—and then
to give away his life . . ." —Matthew 20:27-28,* The Message

Hundreds of scriptural stories reveal the essential truth that our
lives are interwoven, and that we discover ourselves fully in giving
ourselves to others. Scripture suggests that to encounter Jesus Christ
face-to-face in the most tangible way, the whole reality he embodies,
involves serving another person by relieving suffering through feed-
ing the hungry, clothing the naked, visiting the imprisoned, and welcoming the stranger.

Serving others does not merely involve helpful activities that make
a difference; Christ-like service helps us become the persons God created us to be. It fulfills God's hope and will for us.

By serving others, we bear witness that Jesus' reality is true, that
fullness is discovered in the giving and not in the taking; that abundance is found in loving rather than in fearing, that happiness comes
in opening ourselves rather than by closing ourselves off.

The real you, your true self, is discovered in letting Christ lead you
into serving others with compassion. The unsolicited, unconditional
love of God that we receive flows through us to others. As God's love
runs through us, we see Jesus Christ more clearly; we work with him
and he works through us. Serving puts Jesus' love into practice, and
the ultimate reality we see in Christ becomes tangible once again,
revealed as a force and power in the world.

We can serve out of sheer obedience or out of a sense of mutual obligation, or because we find meaning in it. The bottom line remains: in Christ, human suffering requires response. Ultimately, the practice of compassionate service in Christ's name grows from interior decision, a spiritual reorientation. As our life with God becomes more vibrant, dynamic, and real, we discover that we can choose to stand in a place of love, of hope, and of risk with an outward-focused posture; or we can choose to stand in a place of fear, defensiveness, protection, and self-absorption. The more consciously aware we become of our interior life with God, the better choices we make. Growing closer to God draws us closer to one another.

The future belongs to God, and to accept this interpretation of life changes how we think and act, lending hope, urgency, will, and courage to our efforts to follow Christ in serving others. "Your kingdom come; your will be done, on earth as it is in heaven." With this prayer, we offer ourselves afresh to the reign of God.

How we choose makes all the difference. Whom we trust to follow changes everything. What we believe about ultimate reality is pivotal. Meaningful, fruitful service involves the training of the heart. It begins with interior work. The story we choose to tell determines the life we choose to live.

On an impulse, someone contemplating the life and death of Jesus decided to lie down on her back on the grass of an open field with her arms totally stretched out as if on the cross. She remained in that position in a mood of exploring prayer, thinking about how she felt in that position. *Vulnerable.* That was the single word that captured what she was feeling. To follow Jesus Christ involves trusting that a life with greater vulnerability is richer, and that opening ourselves in risky embrace is not irresponsible, but life-giving.

Read John 13:1-17.

What motivates you to serve, to relieve suffering, or to seek justice? Do you delight in doing good or is it a chore? How have you experienced Christ while serving?

Prayer: Make me quick to respond to those in distress, eager to help, and never irritated or discouraged enough to give up, finding you in serving my sisters and brothers.

26

Day Twenty-Six

*"I'm telling the solemn truth: Whenever you did one of these things
to someone overlooked or ignored, that was me—you did it to me."*
—*Matthew 25:40*, The Message

The Covenant Prayer, composed and adapted by John Wesley,
invites complete humility and obedience to God's service, asking God
to work through us or to work around us, and to take us to places and
put us alongside people we would never choose for ourselves.

> I am no longer my own, but thine.
> Put me to what thou wilt, rank me with whom thou wilt.
> Put me to doing, put me to suffering.
> Let me be employed by thee or laid aside for thee,
> exalted for thee or brought low for thee.
> Let me be full, let me be empty.
> Let me have all things, let me have nothing.
> I freely and heartily yield all things
> to thy pleasure and disposal. . . .[8]

"What in the world am I doing here? I can't tell you how many times
I've found myself asking that question." That's how Ken tells about the
unexpected places his faith journey has taken him. Ken is a medical
technician in his mid-fifties, a husband and father, a tennis player, and
a handyman. Ken worked with the youth group on a week-long hous-
ing rehab project. Later Ken received training and led a work team to
Nicaragua where they rebuilt a school damaged by a hurricane. Now
he mentors new members who want to get involved with hands-on

service projects. "I never imagined myself doing this," he says. "But it answers the question, *What in the world am I doing here?* This is the reason God put me here."

Sondra occasionally used her nursing skills to support weekend projects at her urban church that has an active ministry for the homeless, for addicts, and for people living with HIV. She also raised money for her congregation's partner church in Mozambique. When she visited Mozambique, the experience changed her life. African American herself, she became passionate about health issues in Africa and working as an advocate on world health issues and the diseases of poverty. She has helped other people serve the poorest of the poor.

Ken and Sondra followed paths that fit their gifts, context, and passions. With a disciplined pattern of serving and of opening themselves to following Christ, they make a real difference in the lives of others and are changing the part of the world God has given them to transform.

Risk-Taking Mission and Service changes the lives of those who offer ministry. It changes the lives of those who receive ministry. It changes the world as we share directly with God in the creating and re-creating work that makes all things new.

People who practice Risk-Taking Mission and Service understand obedience to Christ. Some things they do because Jesus would do it and invites them to do it. They go where Jesus goes.

They improve on how to have a greater impact. They become progressively more strategic in their service, maximizing effectiveness and fruitfulness. They learn to serve.

They saturate their work with prayer, finding strength, grounding, motivation, and calling in their relationship with God. Through serving, they discover God; through God, they discover serving.

Start anywhere, any time. It is never too late. And with continued cultivation and the passage of time, the difference we make multiplies and the sense of satisfaction we experience deepens. When we answer Jesus' call, "Follow me," there's no predicting where we will end up!

Read Matthew 16:24-26.

When have you moved out of your "comfort zone" in order to help another person? Where is the most unexpected place following Christ has ever taken you?

Prayer: God, help me distinguish between what is merely convenient, easy, and rewarding for me and what is essential for serving others with real love and respect.

27
Day Twenty-Seven

"If you only love the lovable, do you expect a pat on the back? . . . Help and give without expecting a return. You'll never—I promise—regret it."
—*Luke 6:31-36*, The Message

One rainy night I started up the stairs to my seminary apartment when I encountered one of my professors. Dr. D. was one of the most respected theologians of his generation, and I was surprised to see him in a student dorm. Covered by a wet overcoat, he was carrying groceries up the stairs. I offered to help, and as we walked together I heard the story. The wife of a student was undergoing cancer treatment. Dr. D. had visited with them, and offered to help in any way he could. As a result, he went shopping for them after he finished his classes. He'd been doing this for weeks. Nothing I learned from him in the courses he taught had as much personal impact on me as finding him in that staircase on a cold, rainy night.

Service refers to the volunteer impulse animated by the Spirit of God that causes people to offer their time, energy, and leadership to help their congregations and communities thrive. Through service, we become "doers of the word, and not merely hearers" (James 1:22), putting our faith into practice in concrete and visible ways. The church fulfills its mission through service.

Mission turns service outward and extends God's love to the people of the community, the nation, and the world, and refers to the positive difference we make in the lives of others, whether or not they will ever become part of the community of faith. Mission pulls us out of ourselves and connects us with people we don't know.

Jesus pushes us to extend our empathy to those not already in our circle of concern, and invites us to inspire others to do the same. "Here is a simple rule of thumb for your behavior: Ask yourself what you want people to do for you; then grab the initiative and do it for them!" (Luke 6:31, *The Message*). An outward-focused life flows naturally from following Christ, and early followers visited the sick and the imprisoned, provided resources for the poor and vulnerable, reached out to people in need. To live "in Christ" means not only are we sustained by the presence of God's love revealed in Christ, but that the Spirit of Christ permeates us and motivates us to serve.

At the moment we face human suffering, a choice presents itself. If we pay careful attention to our natural tendencies, we want to avoid pain, to deny the problem. But if we listen deep within our soul, we discover that something inside us also draws us *toward* the suffering.

If we move toward suffering rather than running from it, we experience uncomfortable moments and awkward incidents. We risk feeling helpless, and we risk sharing the pain of the person who suffers.

Training the heart to follow Christ involves learning to overcome fear. We acknowledge it and understand it, but choose to live by love instead. Our relationship with God and the community of Christ fosters confidence and hope. Risk-Taking Mission and Service are where courage and joy intermingle.

People who practice Risk-Taking Mission and Service do not think more highly of themselves than they ought to think. They practice humility. The difference they make comes from God.

They treat well those who society thinks it's all right to mistreat. They treat people the way they would want to be treated. They love their neighbors.

They practice serving, and there are no instant experts. They begin small, anticipate feelings of temporary incompetence, and build up their "serving muscles." They practice when it's easier not to, they overcome internal resistance and external criticism, and they serve with others and learn from mentors. They become servants of Christ.

Read 1 Corinthians 13.

Who modeled the life of service for you? What's your earliest memory of helping others as an expression of your faith? Do you currently practice a disciplined pattern of serving others?

Prayer: Lord, help me grab the initiative and treat others as I would want to be treated. Teach me humility, courage, perseverance, discernment, and respect in my following you by serving others.

28

Day Twenty-Eight

"What does the LORD require of you
but to do justice, and to love kindness,
and to walk humbly with your God?" —Micah 6:8

"Justice is love with legs," one seminary professor said. God's love takes a social form when the followers of Jesus learn to love strangers by relieving their suffering.

Victims of violence, poverty, discrimination, and people who suffer through war, famine, or natural disaster often lack the power to effect change that will relieve them. If no one with power and resources speaks for them or stands with them, how can their voices be heard? To *advocate* means to speak for, to act on behalf of, to give support. Among the most important ways followers of Christ express God's gracious love is through advocacy, speaking for those who cannot speak for themselves.

As followers of Jesus, we look at the world through the perspective of someone who suffered innocently, rather than through the lens of privilege, power, and wealth. Christianity began with catastrophic brokenness and violence, resulting in a persevering, sacrificial love that drives us to work on behalf of the suffering with unending passion. We can do no other. To follow Jesus in first-century Palestine meant confronting violence against women, embracing children, exposing self-serving judges, condemning money changers, and challenging the indifference of the wealthy toward the poor and vulnerable. To follow Jesus today involves confronting abuse of power by government officials, challenging corporate greed and unfair labor practices, praying for peace, and supporting healthcare for children. Social change is risky.

Most of us probably do our best to make conscientious choices based on good motives. Yet people can live moral lives while also unknowingly participating in systems that are immoral or hurtful. Part of the hard inner work of perceiving God's activity involves developing a social consciousness, a heightened awareness of how our lives interconnect with others in positive as well as hurtful ways.

In following Christ, one of the greatest risks is the sin of omission, failing to do the things we ought to do. Sometimes we know what is right, but a lack of courage makes us afraid to act. Our self-interest and unwillingness to act are offensive to God.

We are personal disciples and social creatures, and God's grace leads us to private action and public change. God forms us in the way of Christ for the transformation of the world.

Famine is real. Disease is real. Devastating birth defects caused by toxins in the environment are real. Killing is real. Addiction, desperation, violence, and poverty are real.

In a world where these things are real, what kind of person do you want to be? What kind of person do you think God wants you to be?

People who practice Risk-Taking Mission and Service do not avoid the hard tasks, the unsolvable problems, the persistent challenges. They take resistance and disappointment in stride, knowing that if serving people was always easy and convenient, then it wouldn't have taken Christ to teach us, and he wouldn't have told us about taking up crosses.

People who practice Risk-Taking Mission and Service find a way. Nobody is too far away, no resistance too severe that they can't figure out some way to make a positive difference. They connect, collaborate, negotiate, borrow, strategize, and push until a way opens. They mobilize others to meet human needs. They inspire and teach and lead. They do not use guilt or coercion. They help people take the first steps.

They walk gently with those who are vulnerable. They see the face of Christ in those they serve, and they represent the grace of God in their serving. They don't merely pray for peace, they work for it.

Read Luke 4:16-21.

What are three critical issues requiring response and service to improve the human condition and relieve suffering? Where do you see yourself fitting in to make a difference?

Prayer: May I never feel embarrassed to speak for you, Jesus, or to act on the behalf of those who suffer. Remain at my side as you push me toward people who need your sustaining presence. Help me live for others, Christ, as you have lived and died for me.

The Grace of Giving

THE PRACTICE OF EXTRAVAGANT GENEROSITY

Generosity describes the Christian's unselfish willingness to give in order to make a positive difference for the purposes of Christ. *Extravagant Generosity* describes practices of sharing and giving that exceed all expectations and extend to unexpected measures.

Extravagance does not correspond with giving that is merely dutiful, required, burdensome, or simply doing one's part. *Extravagance* denotes a style and attitude of giving that is unexpectedly joyous, without predetermined limits, from the heart, over-the-top, extraordinary, and propelled by great passion. *Extravagant Generosity* is giving to God as God has given to us.

For the next several days, notice generosity—in others, in yourself, from God. And reflect upon the place of money in your life—how it is earned, saved, spent, and given. Think about your family's definitions of success and the sources of happiness. How does God influence your relationship with money, and how does money influence your relationship with God? How does God use our giving to change the world, and to change us?

Strengthen me, O God, for the hard work of being honest with myself as I seek to practice Christ-centered generosity.

29

Day Twenty-Nine

"Giving, not getting, is the way. Generosity begets generosity."
—*Luke 6:38*, The Message

Hundreds of scriptural stories, parables, and verses focus on possessions, wealth, poverty, giving, gifts, offerings, tithes, charity, sacrifice, generosity, and sharing with those in need, providing a strong theological basis for giving.

In the Old Testament, people of faith practiced *first fruits*, the giving of the first and best of the harvest, livestock, or income for the purposes of God. Abram offered up a tithe, or tenth, of everything, and Jacob returned one-tenth of everything to God (Genesis 14:20; 28:22). The Psalms and Proverbs repeatedly encourage the sharing of gifts with God and with the poor. Giving reveals and fosters trust in God.

Jesus teaches that the widow who dropped two coins in the Temple treasury gave more than all the wealthier people because she, out of her poverty, gave all that she had (Luke 21:1-4). And he highlights the foolishness of the farmer who built bigger barns to contain his earthly possessions while neglecting those things that would make him rich toward God (Luke 12:16-21). With his story about Lazarus suffering at the front gate of the rich person's house, Jesus reveals God's disfavor with the wealthy who refuse to help those in need when they have the capacity to do so (Luke 16:19-31). How we use money matters to God.

Zacchaeus, the tax collector and outcast who was transformed by the grace of God when he met Jesus, immediately pledged to give up his ill-gained wealth. Giving is a sign of the changed life. Giving opens our souls to God's lead.

"For God so loved that world that he gave his only Son" (John 3:16). The root of generosity is God's love. We give because God gives.

John Wesley, the founder of Methodism, wrote:

> Do all the good you can,
> By all the means you can,
> In all the ways you can,
> In all the places you can,
> At all the times you can,
> To all the people you can,
> As long as ever you can.

Wesley wrote extensively on the use of money, the danger of riches, and the importance of giving. For Wesley, all things belong to God. This changes how we perceive the manner by which we *earn* money and *save* money, causing us to do so in appropriate ways. And it changes how we *spend* money, making us more responsible, and shapes how we *give* money. Wesley valued industrious and productive work, but he believed that acquiring money does not provide a profound enough life purpose to sustain the human spirit. When he wrote, "Earn all you can, save all you can, and give all you can," he drew an unbreakable link between acquisition and generosity, inviting us to use our material wealth to deepen our relationship with God and to increase our positive impact for God's purposes.

No stories from Scripture tell of people living the God-related spiritual life while fostering a greedy, self-centered, self-serving attitude. Knowing God leads to generosity. Generosity helps us know God.

Read 1 Timothy 6:17-19.

Who first taught you to give? Who models generosity for you? How have your patterns of giving changed as you have matured in faith?

Prayer: You have invited me to give, Lord; now provoke me to greater generosity so that I may discover more of your life in mine.

30

Day Thirty

"They are to do good, to be rich in good works, generous, and ready to share,
thus storing up for themselves the treasure of a good foundation for the future,
so that they may take hold of the life that really is life."
—1 Timothy 6:18-19

Paul and Carolyn have been leaders in their congregation for years, and their generosity has grown steadily as they have matured in faith. They also have enjoyed substantial financial success. When their church felt called to reach more people and younger generations by building a new sanctuary, Paul and Carolyn were challenged to give a major gift. They prayed about it for weeks, before deciding to give the largest gift they had ever given in their lives. "I felt like I was asked to partner with God for a great purpose," Paul said. "Our gift became one of the great delights of our lives. We loved knowing that we could make a difference. We were deeply moved by the experience." Carolyn adds, "If God gives you the capacity and the passion to do something, why in God's name wouldn't you do it?"

People give because generosity helps them achieve God's purposes in *themselves*. By giving, we develop the inner qualities of generosity. Generosity is not a spiritual attribute someone acquires apart from the practice of giving. It becomes discernable only through visible behavior. We cannot become generous and cling to everything we have without letting go. The opposite of generosity is greediness, selfishness. These are not the qualities that lead to life, and so by our giving we cultivate a different nature inside ourselves.

God uses our practice of giving to reconfigure our interior life. By giving, we craft a different inner desire as the driving element of life. Our motivations change.

Giving moderates the powerful and sometimes destructively insatiable drive for acquisition. In the daily interior struggle fostered by a consumerist, materialist society that pressures us to pursue many things that do not lead to real happiness, the practice of giving aims us at what ultimately satisfies. Giving sanctifies and deepens the struggle, and constantly resets the internal compass in the right direction. Generosity becomes a tool God uses to draw us closer to God and to align us more closely with God's desire for us.

Read Mark 12:41-44.

What motivates you to give? How does giving shape your relationship to God? How does your giving influence other aspects of your life? How does God use your giving to influence you?

Prayer: I am your project, Lord. Use my desire to give to create me anew. Never forget me, even when I forget you.

31

Day Thirty-One

"Take care! Be on your guard against all kinds of greed;
for one's life does not consist in the abundance of possessions."
—*Luke 12:15*

Tolstoy, in "How Much Land Does a Man Need?" writes about a man, Pakhom, who farms the land given to him by his father. He wants more, so he saves and sacrifices until he expands his acreage, and even this is not enough. He hears about another region where more land can be bought with less money, so he sells his farm and moves his family across the country to the larger spread. Still, he is dissatisfied. Finally, he hears about a place where the king is offering an extraordinary deal. If you give the king all your money, you may take possession of all the land you can personally encompass by walking around it in a single day. Pakhom imagines how far he could walk in a day, and all the land he could own. He sells all his property and pays the king in exchange for his chance to walk the perimeters of the land that will be his.

A stake is hammered into the ground before sunrise. Pakhom must return to the stake before sunset, and all the land that he circles before that time will be his. As the day dawns, he runs at full speed in order to cover as much territory as possible. As the day heats up, he slows down and begins to circle back, but he sees lush pastures that he must possess, so he extends his path to include them. As the sun moves lower, he realizes that he has miscalculated, and he fears that he may not return to his starting place in time. He runs harder to reach the stake before sunset, pushing himself beyond exhaustion. He comes within view of his destination with only minutes to go. Pushing dangerously beyond his body's capacity to continue, he collapses and dies within reach of the stake.

How much land does a person need? Tolstoy ends his short story by saying that "six feet from head to heel" was all Pakhom needed.[9] Why are we discontent with what we have?

Giving puts us in a healthier relationship with our possessions, and with the material world in which we live. We like making money, but we enjoy other things as well, such as the love of our family; belonging to community; a sense of meaning, accomplishment, contribution, and service. We enjoy making a positive difference in the lives of other people. But how do we maintain balance and perspective? How can we appropriately secure the basic needs of food, shelter, education, and health while also living with purpose? How do we avoid too much preoccupation with the things that do not ultimately satisfy, and cultivate those things that do? The intentional practice of generosity helps us keep our priorities straight.

Giving reflects the nature of God. We give because we are made in the image of God, whose essential nature is giving. We are created with God's nature imprinted on our souls; we are hard-wired to be social, compassionate, connected, loving, and generous. God's extravagant generosity is part of our essential nature as well. But we are anxious and fearful, influenced by a culture that makes us believe we never have enough. God sent Jesus Christ to bring us back to ourselves, and back to God. As we "have in us the mind that was in Christ Jesus," we become free.

Growing in the grace of giving is part of the Christian journey of faith, a response Christian disciples offer to God's call to make a difference in the world. Generosity enlarges the soul, realigns priorities, connects people to the body of Christ, and strengthens congregations to fulfill Christ's ministries.

Read Luke 12:13-21.

Do you sometimes feel that your life consists in the abundance of your possessions? How can practicing generosity counteract greed and begin to balance the priorities of your life?

Prayer: Help me put aside defensiveness and self-deception to look honestly at my giving through your eyes, Lord.

32

Day Thirty-Two

"Every good and perfect gift is from above, coming down from the Father of the heavenly lights." —James 1:17, NIV

Fundamentally, we either consider the material things in our life—our money, house, property—as owned by God and belonging to God, and we manage them for God's purposes, or we view them as owned by us. If they are owned by God, then our tithes and offerings represent our returning to God what belongs to God already. What we keep also belongs to God, and we feel obligated to spend it wisely and not frivolously, and to invest it in ways that do not dishonor God's purposes. We try not to waste money or to live more lavishly than we should. We spend responsibly, allowing our relationship with God to form our minds. We manage God's resources as faithfully as we can.

But if we believe that our material resources fundamentally belong to us and that we entirely possess them ourselves, then we can do whatever we please with what we own, and our tithes and offerings are giving something that belongs to us, to God. God should be grateful for our generosity in giving a percentage for God's purposes rather than our feeling grateful for the privilege of using what belongs to God.

Think about the possession of land. Suppose we hold legal title and own land according to civil authorities. In the larger span of the earth's history, does our patch of soil actually belong to us, or are we temporary stewards? The land didn't begin with us and doesn't end with us. The land we claim to own has existed for millions of years, was used by humans for millennia before us, and will remain for eons more after we are gone. For the ordering of civil life, we rightly say we own the property and it belongs to us. But our mortality assures that we are only the temporary stewards, managers, and keepers. At our dying, what will the things we own mean to us? Whose will they be? People live and perish, but purposes are eternal. With that understanding comes a profound and humble sense of responsibility about how we use the land. It's temporarily ours to enjoy, but we do so with respect and awe, because ultimately everything belongs to God, and not to us.

This concrete example applies to all of the temporal elements of our lives—our possessions, our wealth, even our bodies and minds. Which perspective is truer, more ethically sound, more aligned with reality? That it all belongs to us and we can do whatever we want? Or that we are the temporary beneficiaries, and we find meaning in using what God has entrusted to us to the highest purposes? Which perspective fosters better decisions and deepens a spiritually grounded sense of community and responsibility? The wisdom revealed in Scripture and tradition for more than three thousand years is that those who practice from the perspective of a steward find greater happiness.

The practice of Extravagant Generosity stretches us to offer our utmost and highest to God rather than to give in a manner that is haphazard, unplanned, reactive, minimalist, mediocre, or mechanical. People who practice Extravagant Generosity give with unexpected liberality; they make giving a first priority. They go the second mile. They do not give from a "what remains" mentality, but from a "what comes first" priority. Giving seriously becomes a personal spiritual discipline, a way of serving God, and a means of helping the church fulfill its God-appointed mission. Focused conviction and intention causes them to give in a more pronounced way, without fear and with greater trust. Giving changes their lives.

Read Matthew 25:14-30.

How do you feel about the statement "all things belong to God"? When was a time you felt God transformed your life because you gave? What's the most fun you've ever had giving?

Prayer: Lord, I pray that in you I will break fresh ground in my thinking and doing.

33

Day Thirty-Three

"I have learned to be content with whatever I have. I know what it is to have little, and I know what it is to have plenty. . . . I can do all things through him who strengthens me." —Philippians 4:11-13

Generosity derives from a profound reorientation in our thinking about how we find contentment in life. Paul writes, "I have learned to be content with whatever I have," but Paul was not a slacker, lacking in initiative! He was industrious, competitive, and ambitious for the work of God. Paul realized how seductive our activity and our appetite for more could become. We begin to believe that happiness depends upon outward circumstance and material comforts rather than deriving from inner spiritual qualities—love, peace, compassion, self-control, gentleness, prayerfulness. Possessing greater wealth does not mean that we experience contentedness. We can still feel panic, emptiness, striving, and isolation. We feel needy, and our appetites become insatiable. Surrounded by water, we are dying of thirst.

Breaking the cycle of conditioned discontent requires courageous soul work. Abundant living derives from generative relationships, from mutual support, and from knowing how to love and be loved. Contentment arises from seeking that which satisfies.

Contentedness comes from personal integrity, a life aligned with high values, depth of spirit and of mind, growth in grace and peace. These grant release from agitation, from unhealthy striving, and from continual dissatisfaction. Founded on these, we may value many of the things our culture induces us to seek, but without the harmful, destructive intensity. We want to improve our conditions and standing, but we don't embrace these objectives with the panicked intensity our society would have us do.

Primarily, contentedness is formed in us by the practice of generosity. Contentedness is learning to be happy with what we have rather than feeling distressed by what we lack. In our voluntarily giving away part of our wealth and earnings, we are saying, "I can spend all of this on myself, but I choose not to." In that simple act, repeated and deepened with frequency and intentionality, we break the bonds of self-destructive acquisitiveness.

Second, contentedness results from a deep, cultivated sense of gratitude. Generous people are thankful. They give thanks in all things, and their gratefulness sharpens their awareness of the deeper sources of happiness and from the spiritual awareness that God has already provided us everything we need to flourish. All is grace upon grace.

Finally, contentedness comes from persistent interior work and cooperation with the Holy Spirit to develop the personal habits that keep us from surrendering our sense of well-being, identity, and purpose to materialist measures. Living fruitfully is not merely a matter of having something to live on, but something to live for. Purpose, connection, love, service, friendship, family, generosity—these sustain contentedness.

People who practice Extravagant Generosity live with a sense of gratitude. They give thanks in all circumstances. Love is a gift, and life is grace.

They enjoy giving. They pray and hope and dream about the good they accomplish through their gifts. They consecrate their giving to God. They delight in generosity.

They delight in receiving money, find pleasure in its responsible use, and experience joy in giving to God's purposes. They do not become too attached, and are not stopped, deceived, slowed, misled, or detoured in their following Christ by the possession of money. They are rich toward God.

Read 2 Corinthians 8:1-7.

What causes you to feel content? How do you avoid a self-destructive acquisitiveness? What personal habits help to keep you grounded in Christ?

Prayer: I'm so full of myself sometimes, God. Help me seek you above all things, to offer my best, to be rich in helping others, and to be as extravagantly generous with you as you are with me.

34

Day Thirty-Four

*"This most generous God who gives seed to the farmer that becomes bread for
your meals is more than extravagant with you. He gives you something you
can then give away, which grows into full-formed lives, robust in God, wealthy
in every way, so that you can be generous in every way. . . ."*
—*2 Corinthians 9:11*, The Message

Sarah grew up in a family that practiced tithing, and as a child she
put ten cents in the offering plate from each dollar she received. She
remembers receiving her first paycheck of $56 from her first job as a
teenager, and her sense of achievement and delight when she gave
$5.60 to the church. Now in her forties, Sarah has a high-paying job as
a senior executive, and tithing continues to feel natural, a regular pattern of her life. "I love giving," she says, "and I cannot imagine living
my life or loving God without giving back. Tithing was learned and
practiced so early that I developed the muscle memory for giving.
Like practicing my tennis serve for so many years that I don't have to
think about each step, my giving is part of who I am."

For hundreds of generations, the practice of tithing has sustained
growth in personal generosity. To tithe means to give a tenth, and
involves returning to God ten percent of income. Write down your
income for the month, move the decimal point over one place, and
write a check to the church for the amount you see. Do it first thing
when you are paid, and you discover that the practice dials down
appetites, reshapes priorities, and that all other expenses and needs
will re-adjust. For most people, tithing is not easy. It takes time to learn
and adapt and grow into the practice.

Some people perceive the tithe to be nothing more than a left-over from an Old Testament law-based theology, an arbitrary, technical rule with little relevance for later periods.

And yet Jesus commended the practice, even among the Pharisees whom he criticized for making a show of their self-righteousness. The early church practiced the tithe, and so have Christians in every generation since. John Wesley tithed and expected early Methodists to give regularly and generously at every class meeting and chapel service.

The people we admire and respect for their generous spirits, spiritual wisdom, and deep-heartedness invariably have practiced giving in such an extravagant manner that it has reshaped them. They give extravagantly according to their means, and many beyond their means, and most practice or exceed the tithe. The tithe remains a basic expectation of discipleship.

Tithing provides a theologically and biblically faithful standard that is nominal enough to allow people of nearly any income to meet without imposing great hardship and yet large enough to stretch us.

Tithing provides a concrete way for us to take the words we speak, "God is Lord of my life," and put them into practice. Our commitment becomes tangible; our giving becomes a way of putting God first, an outward sign of an inner spiritual alignment. Tithing is not merely about what God wants us to do, but about the kind of person God wants us to become. Does the giving I now practice help me develop a Christ-like heart?

People who practice Extravagant Generosity grow in the grace of giving. They learn. They take small steps until tithing becomes natural. They deepen their understanding of giving through prayer and Scripture. They give more now than in the past, and will give more in the future than they do today.

They do not wait to be asked. When they see a need, they step forward to meet it, offering their resources as a means to help. They do not give to control the church but to support it. They love to give.

Read Psalm 104.

When was a time you felt God's Spirit move you to give your resources beyond what you had previously practiced? What's the largest gift you have ever given? What motivated you? What resulted from the gift, and how did it affect you?

Prayer: What a wildly wonderful world, God. All that I have comes from beyond myself. Open my heart, receiving and giving, like breathing in and breathing out.

Fruitful Living and Offering God's Love

Fruit refers to what Christ accomplishes through us. Jesus expects our life of faith to make a difference. *Fruitfulness* draws our attention to what results from what we've received, the change of soul and character inside us as well as the change that takes place in the world through us by the Holy Spirit.

And the word *fruit* refers to the way plants reproduce. Fruit contain seeds that multiply and create life apart from the original plant and yet related to it. Through fruit, life passes along to another generation. Fruit is new life. Fruit is growth. Fruit is future.

Offering God's love to another person and inviting someone else into the spiritual life multiplies both the inner qualities of spiritual fruitfulness and the outward impact of service more than anything else we could possibly do. Living fruitfully means not only cultivating the fruit of the Spirit within us but also cultivating spiritual life in others. God uses our growth in grace to transform the world for God's purposes.

During the coming days, focus on the new life God gives you in Christ and the new life God offers others through you. How can we live with such grace that people see Christ in us?

Jesus, cause me to be what you have called me to be
for you: disciple, ambassador, light, servant.

35

Day Thirty-Five

"You did not choose me, but I chose you. And I appointed you to go and bear fruit, fruit that will last. . . ." —John 15:16

Vines, branches, seeds, vineyards, farmers, fig trees, harvests, sowers, soils, weeds, roots. *Fruitfulness* provides a metaphor for many profound aspects of the spiritual life and the Christian journey.

Jesus uses fruitfulness to draw our attention to the impact, the consequence of our life in Christ. He says, "My Father is glorified by this, that you bear much fruit and become my disciples" (John 15:8). Fruit evidences discipleship; following Jesus and fruitfulness are inextricably linked. Disciples bear fruit.

Paul uses similar metaphors to explore inner growth, the fruit of the Spirit—love, joy, peace, patience, kindness, generosity, faithfulness, gentleness, self-control (Galatians 5:22-23). Fruitful living cultivates these essential qualities of soul and character. Fruitfulness refers to the interior growth and the reconfiguration of the soul that becomes visible in outward changes of attitude, behavior, and value. Followers grow in grace.

The quality of effect God has on our inner lives and the resulting outward impact we have on the lives of people around us—these comprise spiritual fruitfulness. When Jesus says, "I am the vine; you are the branches," he reminds us that all our fruit derive from our relationship to God in Christ. Our fruit is God's fruit.

Radical Hospitality. Passionate Worship. Intentional Faith Development. Risk-Taking Mission and Service. Extravagant Generosity.

These are the practices of fruitful living. By repeating and deepening these, we cultivate interior fruit of the Spirit as well as grow in our capacity to serve the world for God's purposes. All are interwoven in practice, with each fostering inner growth and each manifesting outward consequence. However, *receiving God, loving God in return,* and *growing in grace* especially feed inner fruitfulness, while *serving others* and *giving generously* particularly bear fruit in the world around us. Fruitful living changes us inside, and through us transforms the world for God's purposes.

Offering God's love to another person and inviting someone else to follow Jesus multiplies both the inner qualities of spiritual fruitfulness and the outward impact of service more than anything else we could possibly do, bearing fruit beyond what we can fathom. Imagine if as a consequence of your following Christ and your invitation, a few other people explore the spiritual life who otherwise might not have done so. Imagine if these people eventually embrace following Jesus themselves, mature in faith, and make a difference in the world through their service, mission, and giving. Imagine how the people you invite to faith intermingle with the lives of countless other people you do not know. The fruit in your life multiplies in unseen and unknowable ways when we offer God's love. The grace of God is replicated, repeated, and shared. Seeds are scattered, some take root and bear fruit in ways beyond what we can comprehend.

Offering God's love multiplies the fruitful life. By offering Christ, we complete God's grace, the grace we received when we invited God into our lives and made room for him in our hearts. The receptivity that opened our hearts to God opens doors to others. Our lives become a doorway through which people enter into the spiritual life. God with us becomes God through us. As we invite and encourage others into the life of Christ and stimulate their spiritual exploration, we perceive God working through us. We become "ambassadors for Christ, since God is making his appeal through us" (2 Corinthians 5:20). Grace becomes tangible through invitation.

Read Galatians 5:22-26.

You are the fruit of someone else's walk with Christ. Who welcomed and sustained you in your earliest steps toward Christ? Who made God's grace and the fruit of the Spirit tangible and real for you?

Prayer: Thank you, Lord, for your love that would not let go of me and for your grace that searched for me and sought me through friends, family, and strangers. Thank you.

36

Day Thirty-Six

"Don't load yourselves up with equipment. Keep it simple; you are the equipment." —Luke 9:3, The Message

"Do you, as the way opens, share Christ with people who do not know Christ? Do you witness to your faith by letting your life speak?" These questions, adapted from a Quaker covenant, remind us of the gentleness, simplicity, and persistence that underlie effective invitation. Even people who are not particularly open to church are nevertheless open to their friends, and to the experiences that their friends value. The most concrete and personal way God reaches out to invite people into faith is through friends who invite friends. Most people who have no church have at least one friend who practices the faith, and that person provides the most likely pathway to the spiritual journey. Are you that person?

Invitation represents one of the most persistent themes in the teachings of Jesus. He forms his disciples with the words, "Follow me." He initiated conversations with the woman at the well, engaged tax collectors, entered homes, approached sickbeds, and consoled mourners. He had an outward focus, looking to the margins of the crowd to draw people toward God. He did not wait for people to discover him. He moved toward them.

Jesus' most compelling parables portray the initiative of God, a love that searches and seeks and waits and persists and refuses to give up on anyone. The lost sheep, the woman and her coin, the father and his son, the Samaritan and the stranger—all describe an active love that steps toward people. If we want to do what Jesus does, we search, seek, and serve.

Critical actions reveal whether Jesus' followers have embraced the kingdom. "I was a stranger and you welcomed me . . . I was in prison and you visited me" (Matthew 25:35-36). These express an active outward focus. And following Jesus involves being sent to invite others, with this advice: "Don't load yourselves up with equipment. . . . *you are the equipment*" (Luke 9:3, *The Message*).

Key words remind us of our "sentness." *Apostle* comes from the Greek *apostolos*, and means "someone sent out." The word *mission* derives from Latin, and means "to send off." As *disciples* (meaning *learners, followers* of a person or idea), we do the things Jesus did and teach what Jesus taught. Our *mission* is to communicate the love of God, to offer God's grace. Every follower of Christ becomes part of the mission and is sent out as "ambassadors of Christ." We've been assigned a duty and provided a setting, such as our workplace, neighborhood, and family network to seek those who need God's love.

Why do followers of Jesus feel compelled to tell others about God's love? God's love has an initiating quality that searches and seeks and never gives up on anyone. This love propels Jesus' followers to the ends of the earth.

The initiating and invitational posture is essential to discipleship. Invitation completes us—there are depths of the inner life that remain beyond our experience without offering Christ. The receptivity that opens us to God leads us to encourage, welcome, and support others. Invitation continues God's love. In us, the Word becomes flesh once more.

Read Matthew 28.

What place and network of relationships has God given you to serve as Christ's ambassador? How does receptivity toward God lead us to open ourselves to others?

Prayer: Dear Lord, you have embraced me with your unmerited, gracious, and everlasting love. Help me offer that same love to others. Widen my vision. Stretch me. Push me.

37

Day Thirty-Seven

"Let your light shine before others, so that they may see your good works and give glory to your Father in heaven." —Matthew 5:16

A mysterious element of our God-related lives is our frequent unwillingness to invite others in a gentle, authentic, and natural way. It's as if we believe that what we have experienced in our own faith journey is of no value. We have developed an attitude that says, "Let those who know nothing of God's love come to their senses and show up at our place on Sunday morning."

If following Christ involves inviting others to explore the inner life and to discover the riches of God's grace, why the ambivalence?

First, we fear offending people, as if by telling a friend about our serving or the worship we love, we appear judgmental since they do not do these things. We cordon off experiences of worship, service, or prayer from the ordinary sharing of daily life. We avoid the spiritual life.

Second, in a live-and-let-live world, we feel uncomfortable with any notion that we may be imposing our values onto others. To propose universal truth claims from a particular vantage point today sounds arrogant and close-minded. We feel an inexplicable unease with the notion that we have something others need or know something others don't. Self-righteousness offends us.

Third, the thought of praying, preparing, and planning to invite another person into the faith community feels manipulative, artificial, contrived, and utilitarian. Intentionality connotes conniving. The invitation benefits the "inviter" more than the "invitee" as the genuine hospitality of Christ dissolves into a membership drive, a marketing ploy.

We see it as *our* invitation rather than *God's*. We despise self-serving motives.

Fourth, invitation reminds us of negative stereotypes of evangelism done rudely—the street corner preacher screaming invectives at passers-by, or the pushy college roommate constantly shoving religion our way. We want nothing to do with practices that cause others to feel cornered and coerced. We reject pushiness.

Fifth, we find it difficult to offer the invitation in a healthy manner because we don't have many good examples to learn from. Ironically, each of us has come to faith or remained on the journey because of the encouragement of other people, and evidently their disposition toward us was not offensive or coercive. And yet, we hesitate to do for others what has been done for us. We lack models.

What personal qualities attracted us to them? What stimulated our curiosity? What practices supported our inner yearnings and helped us to experience God's grace, and to eventually say *Yes* to God?

For me, the inclination to invite others comes from a deep-rooted place inside. It is grounded in the grace I have experienced, an initiating love that sought and found me, and that brought me God's unconditional love. From the depths of my soul, I desire for people to love and to be loved, to experience a sense of purpose in serving others, and to believe that their life matters. I want people to flourish, and for people to feel that life is worth living and people are worth loving and God is worth trusting. I don't try to force people into a mold. I don't want others to make all the choices I've made. But I want them not to be alone, and to know that God loves them and that the things that matter most—love, hope, peace, purpose—are attainable when we open our hearts to God and follow the way we see in Jesus.

Offer God's love. Invite. Pray about it. Learn about it. Grace received becomes grace given; a way discovered becomes a path offered. Grace becomes real through invitation. What's the greatest gift you have ever given? Perhaps the most life-changing gift you will ever offer to another person is an invitation to life with God. This is the gift immeasurable.

Read Matthew 5:13-16.

What causes you to resist offering God's love to others? If everyone in your congregation offered the same quality and frequency of invitation that you do, would your congregation be growing or declining?

Prayer: The old life is gone; your new life in me flourishes. Use me to persuade others by gentle, persistent love to enter into your love and work.

38

Day Thirty-Eight

"Be ready to speak up and tell anyone who asks why you're living the way you are, and always with the utmost courtesy." —1 Peter 3:15, The Message

The church fulfills its mission at the margins of the congregation, where those who actively follow Christ encounter those who are not a part of the community of faith. Picture a congregation as concentric circles of relationship, with those who know each other well and offer leadership in the middle, those who faithfully volunteer a little farther out, and those who are newer or less active a little farther still. When we reach the edge of the farthest circle we discover on the other side the people who are not a part of a community of faith. The church fulfills its mission at that edge, through *service*—helping, serving, or relieving suffering; and through *evangelism*—inviting, welcoming, and sharing faith. In a healthy church, the boundary is wonderfully permeable, and members readily reach across the edge and new people easily enter into the community. That margin is where the action is. That's where the church fulfills its mission. *Hearers* and *talkers* become *doers* at the margin.

While sitting in an airport lounge that had become crowded because of flight delays, I overheard bits of conversations around me. Two businesswomen in their twenties were sitting near me. One of the women became increasingly concerned by her failed attempts to reach the person she was trying to call. She shared with her colleague that she had planned to get home in time to make one hundred sandwiches to take to a soup kitchen and needed to let the program director know she was delayed. She does this twice a month with her church.

There was a long pause. Then the second woman said, "If you ever need help with that, let me know."

The first woman's face lit up, "That would be so cool. It's a whole different world. I'd love showing you how it works."

Conversion is an intimidating term weighted down with so much baggage that sometimes we overlook how small and incidental a first step toward faith might appear. Personal witness, simply expressed, stimulates first steps.

The woman above offered a simple description of something that matters to her. Her language was natural and yet unapologetically invitational. She let someone look over her shoulder to see what she is working on.

Do I expect that the woman at the airport will show up for the 11 o'clock service next Sunday, join the choir, sign up for a Bible study, and start tithing? No, not at all. But I pray that her curiosity about the spiritual life will deepen enough to take a next step, and that through the positive invitation offered by others, she will find a faith community that helps her grow in the life of grace.

How can we overcome our personal unwillingness to comfortably and consistently invite others into the community of faith and into the life of Christ? When we pray for renewal for our congregations, we can't ask God to do for us what God created us to do for God. Invitation is our mission. Offering God's love is our work.

How do we find our voice, our manner, our way to reach out to others? We don't have to stand on the street corner and scream about Jesus or change our theology. We only need to practice our theology and become an instrument of God's grace! Find your approach and prayerfully discern when the time is right to offer a gentle invitation. A gentle invitation may change someone's life forever.

Imagine if you had one such conversation a month. Imagine if one quarter of your congregation's membership had one such conversation each month. It would change your congregation. It could change the lives of people in your community. It would change you.

Read Matthew 13:1-9.

When was a time you had a conversation about the spiritual life with someone who has no church home? How did the experience affect them? You?

Prayer: Give me the spirit, the grace, the right timing, the right tone, the right words, the ripe moment, Lord, to reveal your love.

39

Day Thirty-Nine

"We are ambassadors for Christ, since God is making his appeal through us . . ." —2 Corinthians 5:20

What is it about your life that would make someone else want to be a follower of Jesus Christ, a person of faith, a part of a congregation?

The purpose of inviting other people to follow Jesus is to help them rediscover love—God's love—and to provide a community that gives sustained focus, energy, and resources to developing the spiritual life. No other community besides the church has as its purpose the deepening of such elements of the human soul as hope, forgiveness, generosity, service, joy, peace, justice, gentleness. Love is the key to unlocking the door to ultimate reality, and in the community of Christ we intentionally practice receiving God's love, loving God in return, and loving others. We invite people into a life of love, surround them with the everlasting arms of God, and encourage them to do the same for others. We love because God first loved us.

To bear witness to Christ involves more than inviting people with words. It means living with such grace and integrity that our lives themselves become appealing to others. The second chapter of Acts reports that people were drawn into the way of life of the followers of Christ. They found Christian practice utterly compelling and irresistibly appealing.

Is this true for us? We are inviting people to reconfigure their interior lives. That's an audacious request. They must see in us qualities that make them think, "I want what you have." People are hungry for something that is going to make a difference, and they want to be part of something that matters. Do they see in us "the mind that was in Christ"?

John Wesley, the founder of Methodism, said

> Never dream of forcing [other people] into the ways of God.
> Think yourself, and let think. . . . Even those who are farthest
> out of the way never compel to come in by any other means
> than reason, truth, and love.[10]

The people we admire and respect and who have loved us into the faith are not perfect and neither are we. Followers of Christ sometimes overcome things; other times they feel stuck and small and alone. They doubt and hurt and question. They are persons of faith set on a journey toward Christ whose way they can't always clearly see.

But through intentional practice, they move forward; community gets them unstuck. They tap interior resources that give them strength. They set their lives upon a foundation. They face disappointment and loss just like everyone else, but they cultivate threads of connection to God and other people that pull them through. God uses their disciplined intentionality to change them.

Are we living the kind of life that would make others want to live like us?

Witness is more than verbal invitation. It is a way of life that invites God to work through us.

Read Luke 10:1-11.

What is it about your life that would make someone else want to be a follower of Jesus Christ and be involved in a faith community?

Prayer: You have poured out your life so generously in Christ, restored me to you, given me back my life, and promised the eternity of love. Thank you, Lord Jesus.

40

Day Forty

Mary Magdalene went and announced to the disciples, "I have seen the Lord";
and she told them that he had said these things to her. —John 20:18

Those who offer Christ realize that the journey begins with a personal relationship, leads to a comfortable invitation to a ministry of the church, and results in an embracing of the spiritual life. They trust God's time. A visit to church represents a brush with the body of Christ. They invite.

People who invite others train themselves to feel comfortable talking about spirituality and the interior life with outsiders. They practice until speaking of faith feels natural.

They speak with humility, sharing their faith struggles as well as their trust in matters of the spirit. They speak of new life in Christ in real, authentic, and honest terms. They get themselves out of the way.

They pray about particular people. They prepare themselves for when the moment is ripe for invitation. They ask God's guidance to notice when the way opens.

Encouraging new people toward Christ enriches their own spiritual life. They humbly accept the gift of serving as an ambassador of Christ. A judgmental attitude closes people out and cuts off dialogue. They view people through God's eyes. They rule no one out.

They trust God's time, realizing that the journey is a process that begins with personal relationship and giving people space.

People who consciously bear witness to Christ attend to small actions. They listen when no one else seems to care and take time when everyone else rushes on. God uses simple expressions of grace to incrementally pry open the human heart.

They believe that the church is the body of Christ and a principal means of grace.

Some specifically train in order to offer God's love in unusually hard circumstances, such as with victims of crime, those suffering grief, refugees, the homeless. They go where they know Jesus would go. Reaching others is not about membership numbers or the survival of the institution, but about connecting people to the risen Christ. Their only motive is Christ.

People who offer Christ realize that new life is a journey of a thousand incremental steps; everyone moves toward Christ at different paces. Pathways to Christ are many.

Christ's invitational nature pervades all their work. They involve outsiders in the work of serving the poor and weave those they serve into the community of faith. Their approach is other-centered. They listen more than they speak.

They do not postpone, avoid, resist, or deny the importance of offering God's love. They never force, coerce, insist, or misuse the name of God to instill fear or guilt as tools to pressure people. "Grace upon grace" is their means. God makes ready the human heart; they trust the grace of God.

Our experiencing grace and following Christ remain incomplete until the love of God flows through us into others. We know half the truth if we entirely understand grace according to what we receive. If grace gets in, but can't get out, then we diminish our capacity to grasp what God has entrusted to us. The risen Christ brings new life to us, and through us.

Offering Christ completes us, and accomplishes God's purpose. Opening ourselves to God's grace involves opening the treasure for others, and inviting them in. Inviting God into our hearts leads to inviting others into the heart of God. Radical Hospitality toward God becomes Radical Hospitality toward others.

Read John 20.

How do people see in you how important the decision to follow Christ has been for you? How do people see the risen Christ in you?

Prayer: I give you my hands, my heart, my hope, Lord. Use the change in me to change others for you. May your life be seen in mine.

Changed From the Inside Out

"Take your everyday, ordinary life—your sleeping, eating, going-to-work, and walking-around life—and place it before God as an offering. Embracing what God does for you is the best thing you can do for him. Don't become so well-adjusted to your culture that you fit in without even thinking. Instead, fix your attention on God. You'll be changed from the inside out."
—*Romans 12:1-2*, The Message

Through the personal practice of *Radical Hospitality*, we open ourselves to God's unconditional love, and make room in our hearts for God's grace. We cultivate receptivity; we invite God in.

With patterns of *Passionate Worship*, we love God in return, allowing God to change our hearts, learning to love what God loves and to see the world through God's eyes.

Through the practice of *Intentional Faith Development*, we cooperate with the Holy Spirit in our own spiritual maturation and follow Christ more nearly.

We discern God calling us to make a difference in the lives of others through the practice of *Risk-Taking Mission and Service*.

Eventually, we realize that all that we have and all that we are belongs to God, and we practice *Extravagant Generosity*.

These Five Practices of Fruitful Living, as we repeat and deepen them, shape our perceptions, attitudes, and behaviors. They change us. We grow in grace and in the knowledge and love of God. And we cannot help but share what we have discovered; we offer God's love to others.

The five are a *set* of practices—intertwined, interactive, and interdependent. Progress on one pulls us forward in another. Learning in one area supports growth in all areas. They fit together and complement one another.

The ordered listing may lead us to conceptualize the practices as sequential steps or as a linear progression, and yet growing in grace seldom happens so straightforwardly. God's Spirit is free of the sequences we use to describe its presence.

The same is true with the Five Practices. In fruitful living, the order is pleasantly irregular and surprisingly unpredictable. Fold them gradually into patterns of living. Cultivate them. Accept a gentle sense of urgency about the direction, but patience about the progress.

How do we have the mind in us that was in Christ Jesus? How do we cultivate a life that is abundant, fruitful, purposeful, and deep? How do we live a genuinely good life that pleases God, and makes a positive difference? Spiritual practice answers these questions.

The flourishing life results from repeating and deepening these practices, from the lifelong project of cooperating with the Holy Spirit. As we learn to listen for God and to invite God in and to work with God, our lives are shaped. We become new creations in Christ, and we arrive at places we never expected.

Everybody already worships something, whether we are conscious of it or not. Habits and practices already form us, purposefully or without conscious intent. Society cultivates appetites for exactly the things that do not ultimately satisfy. We unthinkingly adopt these values when we make no conscious choices; these are our gods unless we open ourselves to something deeper.

Through the Five Practices, we worship what is worthy. We choose what satisfies. We accept a deeper serenity. The practices focus us. They represent sustained obedience in a consistent direction, a daily honoring and serving God. They help us stay in love with God.

To find and follow Christ and to serve him—that is fruitful living. These practices are a way forward, tested and true. They show us a way.

To be a follower of Jesus is to take this path, to step by step grow into the life that really is life. God through Christ reveals the way, invites us along, and walks with us. Following Christ will change you; and through you, God will change the world.

Notes

[1] Carl Koch, *Garden of a Thousand Gates: Pathways to Prayer* (Saint Mary's Press, 1998).

[2] All Tillich quotes and references are from his sermon, "You Are Accepted," contained in Paul Tillich's *The Shaking of the Foundations* (Charles Scribner's Sons, 1948); pp. 161–162.

[3] For further discussion of this paradox and the trends and sources of happiness, see Dick Meyer's book *Why We Hate Us: American Discontent in the New Millennium* (Three Rivers Press, 2009).

[4] Joe Eszterhas, *Crossbearer* (St. Martin's Press, 2008); pp. 3–5.

[5] John Wesley, *The Works of John Wesley* on compact disc, Vol. 8, "A Plain Account of the People Called Methodists" (Providence House Publishers, 1995); p. 260, paraphrased.

[6] Wesley, Vol. 5, Sermon 24 "Sermon on the Mount"; p. 296.

[7] Frederick Buechner, *Wishful Thinking* (HarperSanFrancisco, 1993); p. 119.

[8] *The United Methodist Hymnal* (The United Methodist Publishing House, 1989); p. 607.

[9] Leo Tolstoy, *How Much Land Does a Man Need? and Other Stories* (Penguin, 1993); p. 110.

[10] Wesley, Vol. 5, Sermon 37 "The Nature of Enthusiasm"; p. 478.